Double Club

MATHS
Pupil Book 3

Hilary Koll, Steve Mills
and Tom Watt

Rising Stars UK Ltd, 22 Grafton Street, London W1S 4EX

www.risingstars-uk.com

Published 2009

Story author: Tom Watt
Educational authors: Hilary Koll and Steve Mills
Publisher: Jean Carnall
Cover design: Burville-Riley Partnership
Design: Seamonster Design
Illustrations: Seamonster Design/David Woodroffe
Photographs: Getty Images/iStock Photo

Graph data, p55, source: Deloitte, from http://news.bbc.co.uk/1/hi/business/7423254.stm

British Library Cataloguing in Publication Data.
A CIP record for this book is available from the British Library.

ISBN: 978-1-84680-513-4

Printed by Craftprint International Ltd, Singapore

Rising Stars would like to thank Scott Cohen and Alan Sefton of Football in the Community for Arsenal Football Club for their help and support.

Contents

SPORT

July 22 • Daily News

STAYING UP? WAGES UP?

Shelby boys get their reward – exclusive!

Shelby Town's players have proved they are good enough for the Premier League. They are off on holiday now before training in August for a second season in the top flight. Dave Morgan and company got some good news before they headed for the beach. Chairman Ernie Carstairs announced that every member of the squad would get a 10% pay rise for next season.

'The boys did so well for us and we think it's a good investment,' said Carstairs. 'We want to keep this team together and happy at Manor Park.

I understand that the average Premier League wage is now about £32 000 a week. We can't afford those kinds of salaries. But we've got lads here who are wearing the shirt with pride and being paid only a tenth of that. We have to move on!'

Skipper Dave Morgan spoke earlier today on behalf of the team. 'We're delighted,' he said. 'It's not just about money with our lads. I remember when I first signed for Town. I was getting £320 a week plus expenses. I'd have been better off in an office job! But it's great to know the club recognises what we've achieved. Like I say: £320 a week, £3200 a week or £32 000 a week. That's not what matters. It's about keeping Shelby Town where we belong – in the Premier League!'

Team Talk

 How are the numbers £32 000, £3200 and £320 related to each other?

 What other numbers are also related to them? How are £3.20 or £0.32 related to them?

4

Warm Up

▶ **Use place value to multiply or divide whole numbers and decimals by 10, 100 and 1000 and explain the effect**

Chairman, Ernie Carstairs, is doing some accounts. Use the grid to help you answer these questions.

Chairman's Message
When multiplying by 10, 100 or 1000, move each digit one, two or three places to the left. When dividing by 10, 100 or 1000, move each digit one, two or three places to the right.

	Th	H	T	U	t	h
1 £29 x 10 =				2	9 .	
2 £5100 ÷ 10 =	5	1	0	0 .		
3 £0.77 x 100 =			7	0 .	7	7
4 £680 ÷ 100 =		6	8	0 .		
5 £1.33 x 1000 =	1	3	3	1 .	3	3
6 £450 ÷ 1000 =		4	5	0 .	4	5
7 £75 ÷ 100 =			7	5 .	7	5
8 £3.68 x 10 =			3	3 .	6	8

Skills Practice 1

▶ **Find simple percentages of numbers and express tenths and hundredths as percentages**

1 This season, the players' wages are to increase by one-tenth (10%).
  Divide each number by 10 to find how much extra each player will get.
  Then work out how much they will get altogether and write this amount in words.

a)	Chris Jones	£590 000	b)	Dotun Odegbame	£825 000
c)	Peter Jenks	£1 250 000	d)	Al Sefton	£996 500
e)	Peter Ball	£1 115 000	f)	Danny Smith	£1 450 000

2 This season, the backroom staff's wages are to increase by one-hundredth (1%).
  Divide each number by 100 to find how much extra each member of staff will get.
  Then work out how much they will get altogether and write this amount in words.

a)	Bill Simpson	£20 000	b)	Peggy Ellis	£18 000
c)	Nisha Doshi	£19 500	d)	Diane Eastham	£22 800
e)	Sandy Lane	£29 250	f)	Phil Miles	£27 375

Skills Practice 2

▶ **Use efficient written methods to multiply and divide integers and decimals**

Chief Executive, Jane Saunders, is working out how much to pay the staff at the Shelby Town Shop for the hours they have worked during one week, so she makes a list. Work out how much must be paid in total. Do not use a calculator.

> 7 people need to be paid £320 each.
>
> 5 people need to be paid £570 each.
>
> 1 person needs to be paid for working 8 hours at £5.80 per hour.
>
> 3 senior staff need to be paid for working 6 hours at £8.75 per hour.

Game On

These players are saying how much they earn on average per month, per week, per day, per hour, per minute, per second. They assume they are being paid for every month, week, day, hour, minute or second of the year, not just the actual hours they work.

Talk to a friend about which player you think earns the most money in a year.
Now use a calculator to find out how much each player earns in a year.

David Dove I earn £93 000 per month.   **Timmo Hannesen** I earn £21 500 per week.

Stuart Dolan I earn £2700 per day.   **Tom Allenby** I earn £105 per hour.

Bradley Dunne I earn £2.20 per minute.   **Jim MacDonald** I earn 4p per second.

Chairman's Message
Remember these relationships.

1 year = 12 months	1 year = 52 weeks	1 year = 365 days
1 day = 24 hours	1 hour = 60 minutes	1 minute = 60 seconds

The Big Match – Cheque Please!

Play this game with a partner. You will need a dice, some paper and a pencil to keep score.

Kick-off

Key

- Each player should choose one of the cheques below.
- Each player should roll the dice once.
- Find what calculation to do using the key.
- Record your results, e.g. 3000 ÷ 100 = £30
  £3 x 1000 = £3000
- Score a point if both your answers are the same.
- How long will it take you to score 6 points?

x 10   ÷ 10

x 100      ÷ 100

x 1000      ÷ 1000

Date	Shelby Bank	
	Pay Dave Morgan	Date
	Three hundred	£300 000
£	thousand pounds	
		Ernest Carstairs

Date	Shelby Bank	
	Pay Derek Hardaker	Date
	Thirty thousand	£30 000
£	pounds	
		Ernest Carstairs

Date	Shelby Bank	
	Pay Nishi Doshi	Date
	Three thousand	£3000
£	pounds	
		Ernest Carstairs

Date	Shelby Bank	
	Pay Phil Miles	Date
	Three hundred	£300
£	pounds	
		Ernest Carstairs

Date	Shelby Bank	
	Pay Diane Eastham	Date
	Thirty pounds	£30
£		
		Ernest Carstairs

Date	Shelby Bank	
	Pay Graham Hicks	Date
	Three pounds	£3
£		
		Ernest Carstairs

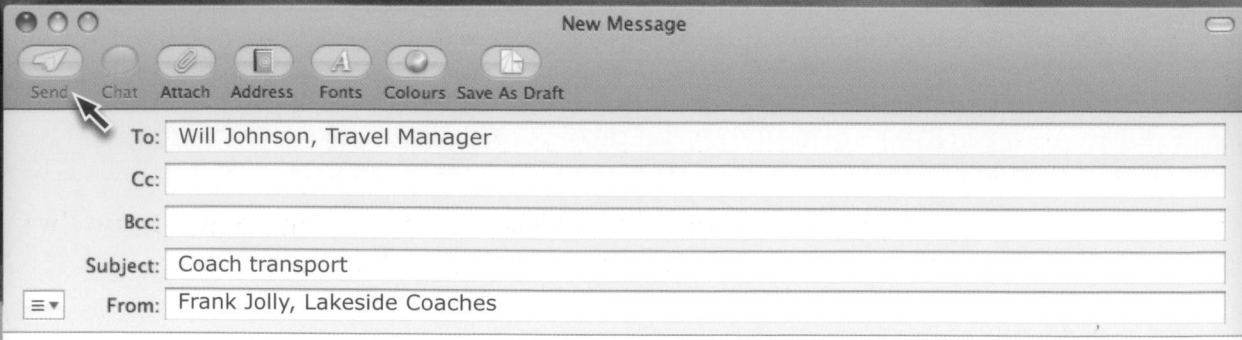

New Message

Send Chat Attach Address Fonts Colours Save As Draft

To: Will Johnson, Travel Manager

Cc:

Bcc:

Subject: Coach transport

From: Frank Jolly, Lakeside Coaches

Hi Will,

Congratulations on the draw at Newcastle. That's another season at least of away trips in the Premier League! Hope you'll be using us again. I think we're still the best value around as far as coach transport is concerned. All the lads are now Town fans. Our drivers all say your boys are a great bunch to be around!

As requested, that breakdown of the cost for the trip to St James' Park last weekend.

Coach hire	£300
Drivers	£250
Fuel	£74.24
TOTAL	**£624.24**

Fuel costs calculated as follows

Distance:	508 miles
Diesel used:	58 litres
Cost per litre:	£1.28
Total cost of fuel:	£74.24

Hope that's what you needed. Any more info I can provide you with, give me a ring in the office. Up the Town!

Regards,

Frank Jolly

Team Talk

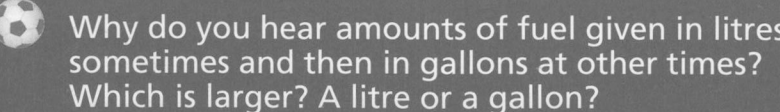

⚽ Why do you hear distances given in miles sometimes and then in kilometres at other times?
Which is larger? A mile or a kilometre?

⚽ Why do you hear amounts of fuel given in litres sometimes and then in gallons at other times?
Which is larger? A litre or a gallon?

Warm Up

▶ **Use efficient written methods to add whole numbers**

Jim, the team's coach driver, keeps a record of the distances he travels to away matches during the season. These are the distances he has travelled so far this season.

Newcastle United match	508 miles
Manchester City match	230 miles
Chelsea match	106 miles
Middlesbrough match	396 miles

What is the total distance he has travelled to away matches so far this season?

Skills Practice 1

▶ **Understand and use decimal numbers and use addition with decimals to 2 places**

▶ **Solve mathematical problems, identifying necessary information**

Jim keeps all his receipts when buying diesel for the coach.
What is the total cost of the fuel he has bought this week?

SESO Manor Park Road Shelby Town	**PB** Sheldon Road Shelby Town	**SESO** Manor Park Road Shelby Town	**PB** Sheldon Road Shelby Town
25/8/08	26/8/08	27/8/08	28/8/08
PUMP 2 Diesel 478 litres	PUMP 8 Diesel 490 litres	PUMP 4 Diesel 465 litres	PUMP 5 Diesel 473 litres
TOTAL (Inc Vat) **£621.40**	**TOTAL** (Inc Vat) **£632.10**	**TOTAL** (Inc Vat) **£595.20**	**TOTAL** (Inc Vat) **£610.17**
www.seso.co.uk	www.pb.co.uk	www.seso.co.uk	www.pb.co.uk

Manager's Message
To add the prices, write them in a vertical list making sure the digits line up correctly.

Skills Practice 2

▶ **Use efficient written methods to subtract whole numbers and decimals**

Jim notes the milometer reading of the coach as he leaves Shelby Town to go to a match and then when he returns.

Work out how many miles he drove on each of these journeys.

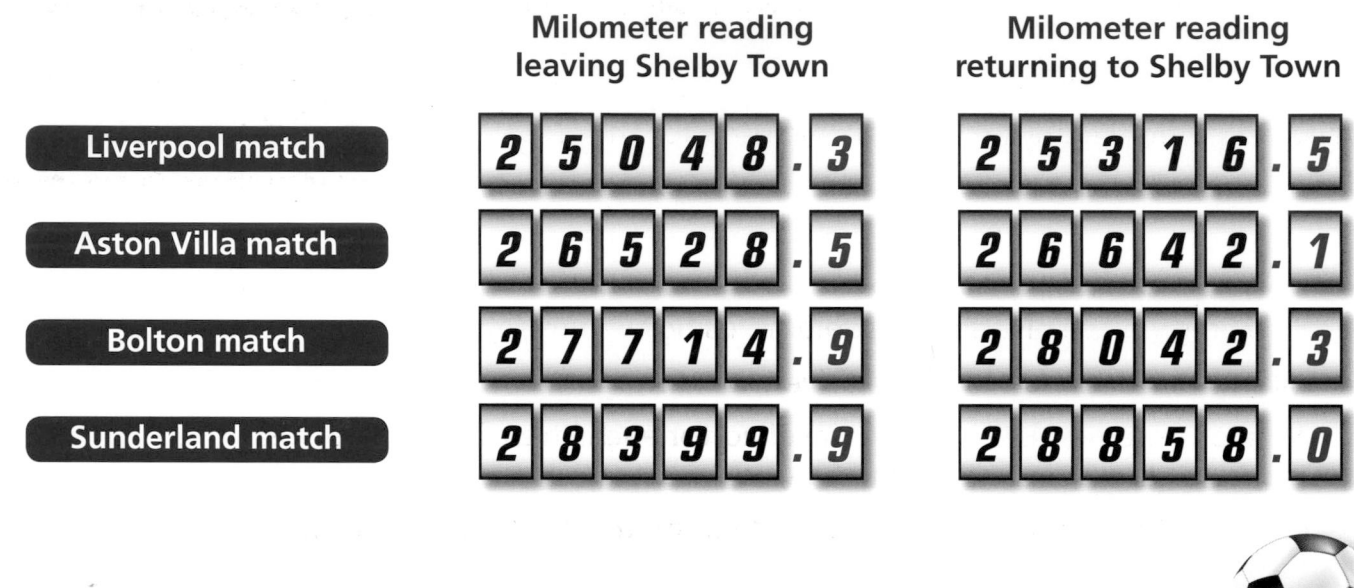

	Milometer reading leaving Shelby Town	Milometer reading returning to Shelby Town
Liverpool match	2 5 0 4 8 . 3	2 5 3 1 6 . 5
Aston Villa match	2 6 5 2 8 . 5	2 6 6 4 2 . 1
Bolton match	2 7 7 1 4 . 9	2 8 0 4 2 . 3
Sunderland match	2 8 3 9 9 . 9	2 8 8 5 8 . 0

Game On

The fuel tank of the coach holds up to 500 litres. Today, Jim knows he needs to put in 480 litres of diesel to fill it up.

PB Diesel **111p** per litre

SESO Diesel **134p** per litre

How much will he save by going to the PB garage rather than the SESO garage?

The Big Match – Miles Per Litre

You will need a calculator for this activity.
Jim recorded the milometer reading for travelling to and from the Portsmouth away match.

	Milometer reading leaving Shelby Town	**Milometer reading returning to Shelby Town**
Portsmouth match	3 6 8 6 9 . 7	3 7 1 3 5 . 2

He also noted how many litres of fuel he used for this trip.

91.4 LITRES

Kick-off

- Work in pairs to solve these problems, using the information above.
- Calculate the number of miles driven on the trip.
- Work out the number of miles travelled for each litre of fuel (miles per litre). Round your answer to 1 decimal place.
- Work out the approximate number of kilometres travelled per litre. Round your answer to 1 decimal place.

> **1 mile is about 1.6 km**

- Use your answer for the number of miles travelled for each litre of fuel. Work out the approximate number of miles per gallon. Round your answer to the nearest mile.

> **1 gallon is about 4.5 litres**

Extra Time

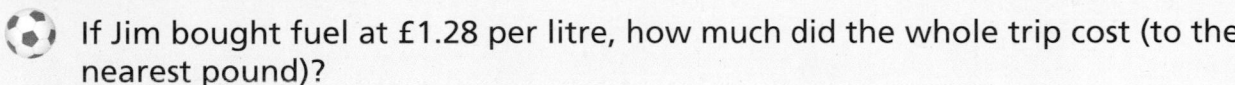

- If Jim bought fuel at £1.28 per litre, how much did the whole trip cost (to the nearest pound)?
- How much is the cost per mile?

NOW SPORTS

Dougie Ball (Studio Presenter): Well, it's a big night for international friendlies. With England's David James injured, who'll come in to replace him against Italy? Let's get a keeper's view on it. We can cross to Manor Park and speak to Shelby Town's Jim MacDonald. Hi, Jim.

Jim MacDonald: Hi, Dougie.

Dougie: Disappointed to have missed out on the Scotland squad again, Jim?

Jim: The boss is looking for a younger keeper, maybe. They know where I am, anyway! I'll just keep doing my best for Shelby Town.

Dougie: You've had a great season, Jim. Getting yourself a bit of a reputation in one against ones!

Jim: Oh, that's always been part of my game. I enjoyed Maths at school and all that work about angles stuck with me! Comes in handy narrowing the angle when a striker's heading towards you.

Dougie: You make the goal look as small as possible behind you?

Jim: Something like that. I practise a lot on where to be standing to give the forward as little of the goal to aim at as possible.

Dougie: Well, it seems to be working! Sorry, Jim. Just got to break off for a minute. Team news from the early kick-off at Windsor Park, then straight back to Jim at Manor Park for his views on England's goalkeeping options …

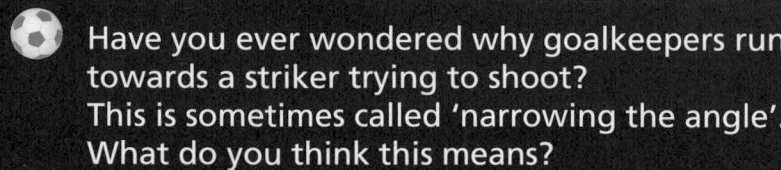

Team Talk

⚽ Have you ever wondered why goalkeepers run towards a striker trying to shoot?
This is sometimes called 'narrowing the angle'.
What do you think this means?

⚽ What is an angle?
Where are the angles on a football pitch and why are they important to a goalkeeper?

Warm Up

▶ Recall division facts and derive other related facts including multiples of 10 and 100

▶ Know that angles are measured in degrees and that one whole turn is 360°

1 Answer these questions.

a) 360 ÷ 2   b) 360 ÷ 3   c) 360 ÷ 4   d) 360 ÷ 6   e) 360 ÷ 9

f) 360 ÷ 20   g) 360 ÷ 30   h) 360 ÷ 40   i) 360 ÷ 60   j) 360 ÷ 90

2 Now use your answers to find

a) how many 20° angles are in a full turn   b) how many 30° angles are in a full turn

c) how many 40° angles are in a full turn   d) how many 60° angles are in a full turn

e) how many 90° angles (right angles) are in a full turn

Skills Practice

▶ Use a protractor to measure and draw angles

▶ Know the sum of angles in a triangle

On the training ground, players are doing some passing drills.

1 Use a protractor to measure each marked angle accurately.

2 Now add up the three angles in each triangle. What do you notice about the totals?
Use this to check your answers.

Game On

A striker is standing in front of the goal with only the goalkeeper to beat. He decides to shoot. At this point he has a 'scoring angle' where, as long as the shot doesn't go over the bar, he can score.

scoring angle = *a* + *b*

These diagrams show the goalkeeper in different positions after running towards the striker as seen from above.

1 Measure the scoring angle in each diagram.

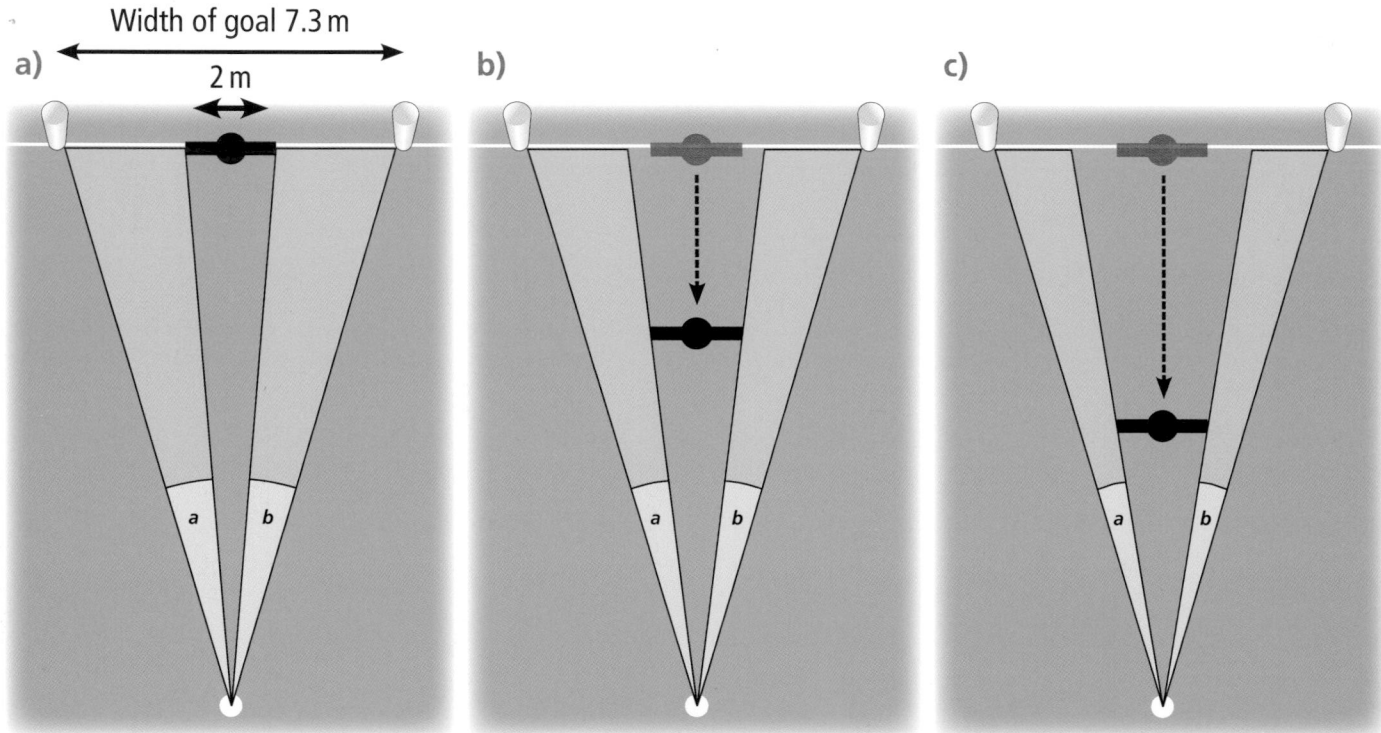

a) Width of goal 7.3 m
   2 m

b)

c)

2 Talk to a partner about why a goalkeeper tends to run towards the striker.
   Why might it not be sensible for the goalkeeper to run too far towards the striker?

The Big Match – Pass It!

Play this game with a partner. You will need a pen, pencil, protractor, ruler and a sheet of plain paper each.

Kick-off

- Draw two dots about 15 cm apart at the bottom of your sheet, in pen, to represent two Shelby Town players. Draw a straight line from dot to dot to show the line of the ball when one player passes it to the other.

- In pen, draw nine other dots on the paper to represent the rest of the Shelby Town team.

- Take turns to choose an angle, e.g. 60° or 72°.

- Both players should draw this angle from one end of their line. Use pencil. You can start the angle from either end of the line.

- If your pencil line reaches one of your players, the pass was successful and you score a point.

- Keep choosing different angles to draw, rubbing out previous angles if you need to.

- The winner is the first player to score five points.

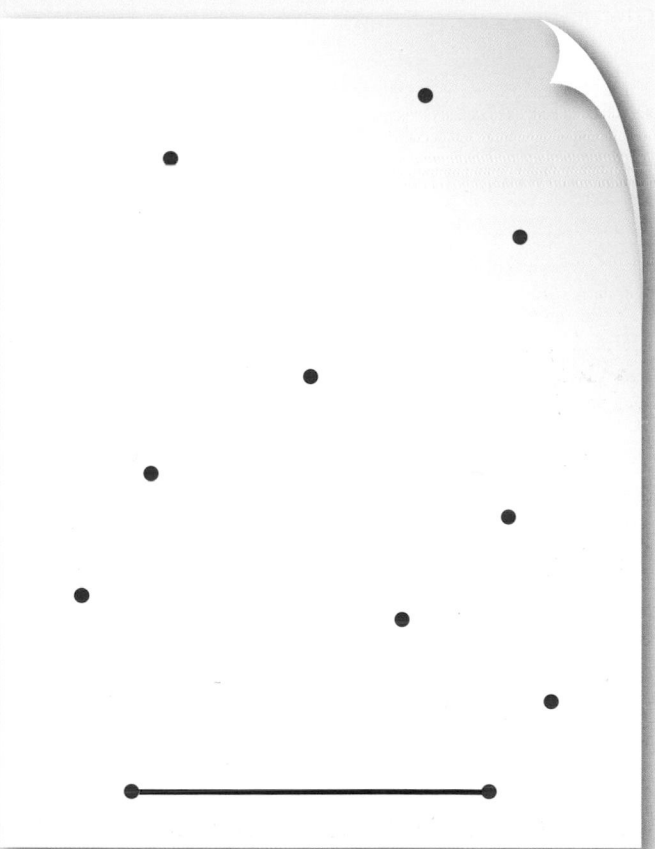

GP Practice
July

JUST CALL HER 'THE DOC'

Shelby GP steps up to the first team!

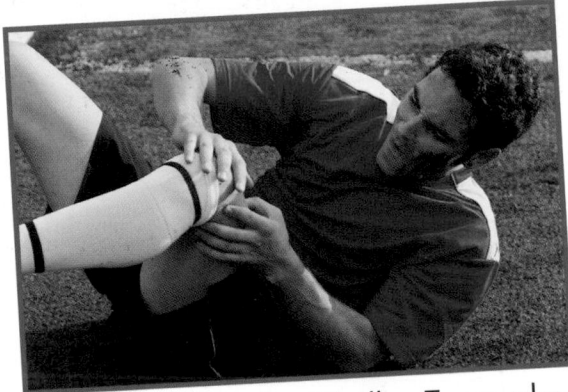

If you've ever seen Shelby Town play, you might recognise Dr Jean Kingston. She doesn't play for the new Premier League outfit, of course. But she's an essential part of the Manor Park team and one of Shelby's best-known GPs.

'I love it,' smiles Jean. 'I've been a Town fan for years. When the chance came along to be club doctor, I took it.

I don't like seeing anyone hurt but it's a thrill running out in front of 30 000 people to check on an injured player!'

Dr Kingston's duties on match day, though, make up only a small proportion of her Town duties. She is a consultant at Manor Park and has to divide up her time carefully.

'I need to check the progress of injured players, advise on treatments and rehab work, and I also do some more general work on health with the younger lads. Prevention is always better than cure.'

She's been keeping patients in Shelby healthy for years. Now, Jean Kingston is making sure the football team's fit for life in the Premier League, too!

Team Talk

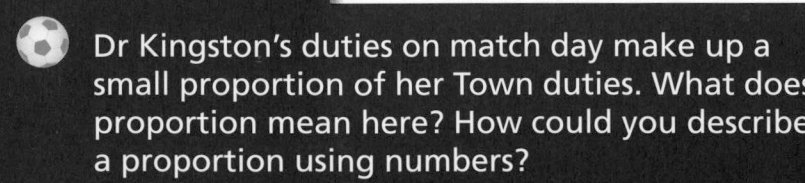

Dr Kingston's duties on match day make up a small proportion of her Town duties. What does proportion mean here? How could you describe a proportion using numbers?

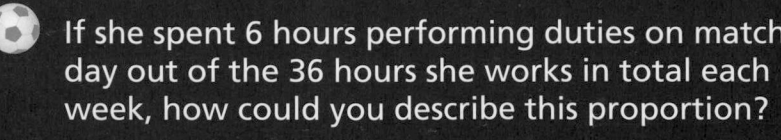

If she spent 6 hours performing duties on match day out of the 36 hours she works in total each week, how could you describe this proportion?

Warm Up

▶ Recall quickly multiplication facts up to 10 x 10

The Shelby Town doctor, Jean Kingston, gives out medication to players and staff for a range of different treatments.

How many tablets should there be in each pot?

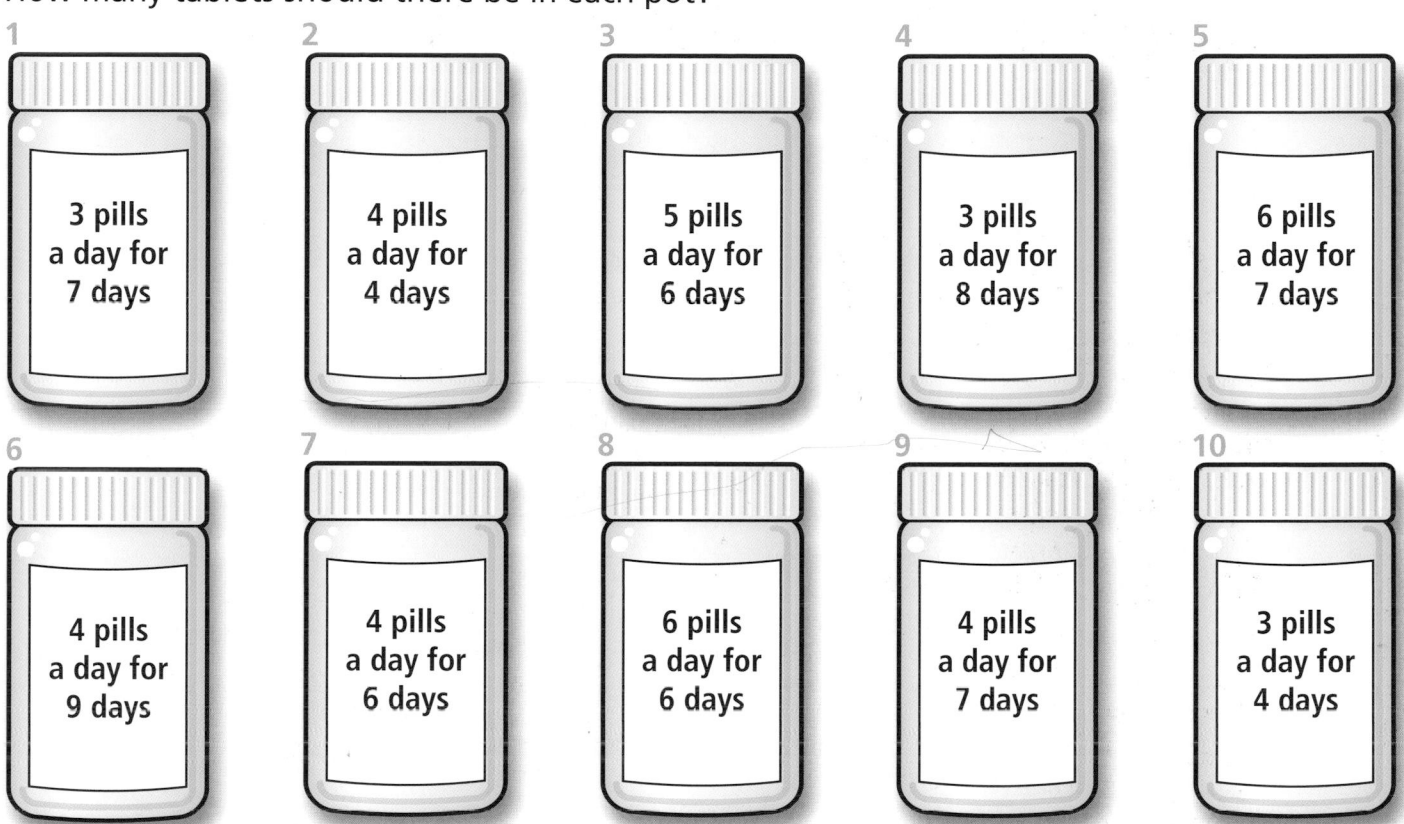

1
3 pills a day for 7 days

2
4 pills a day for 4 days

3
5 pills a day for 6 days

4
3 pills a day for 8 days

5
6 pills a day for 7 days

6
4 pills a day for 9 days

7
4 pills a day for 6 days

8
6 pills a day for 6 days

9
4 pills a day for 7 days

10
3 pills a day for 4 days

Skills Practice 1

▶ Calculate fractions of quantities; relate fractions to multiplication and division

During one week at the club, Dr Kingston works for 36 hours.

- $\frac{1}{4}$ of her time is spent working with the physiotherapists
- $\frac{1}{12}$ of her time is spent giving a first aid talk to staff
- $\frac{2}{6}$ of her time is spent treating the first team
- $\frac{2}{9}$ of her time is spent treating the youth team and reserves
- $\frac{1}{9}$ of her time is spent writing up reports

How many hours did she spend on each activity?

Skills Practice 2

▶ Simplify fractions by cancelling common factors

Dr Kingston uses this table when giving players injections to help relieve pain or to treat certain conditions.

The table suggests what fraction of a full dose should be given to players of different body weights.

	Body weight in kilograms						
	Less than 70 kg	70 kg – 74 kg	75 kg – 79 kg	80 kg – 84 kg	85 kg – 89 kg	90 kg – 94 kg	95 kg or over
Fraction of dose	$\frac{3}{9}$	$\frac{12}{32}$	$\frac{10}{24}$	$\frac{18}{24}$	$\frac{25}{30}$	$\frac{42}{48}$	full dose

Simplify each of the fractions to make the table easier to use.

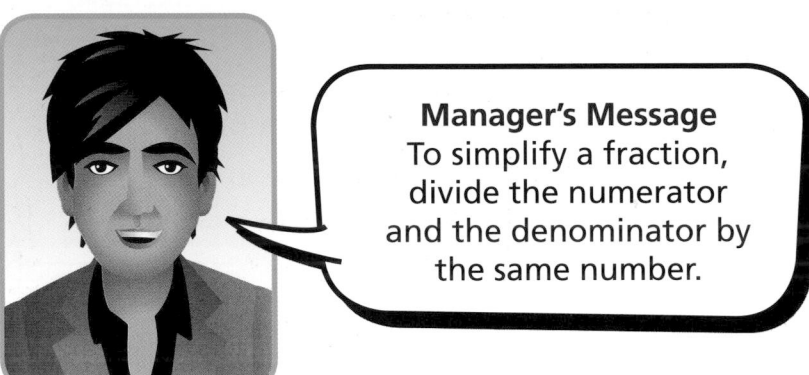

Manager's Message
To simplify a fraction, divide the numerator and the denominator by the same number.

Game On

If a full dose is 4.8 ml, work out the dose for each player.

1 **Stuart Dolan** I weigh 67 kg.

2 **Pierre Jean Vert** I weigh 84 kg.

3 **Peter Jenks** I weigh 90 kg.

4 **Dotun Odegbame** I weigh 77 kg.

5 **Dave Morgan** I weigh 88 kg.

6 **Danny Smith** I weigh 73 kg.

Which players would be given a dose exactly twice the amount for another player?

The Big Match – Fraction Action

Work with a partner.

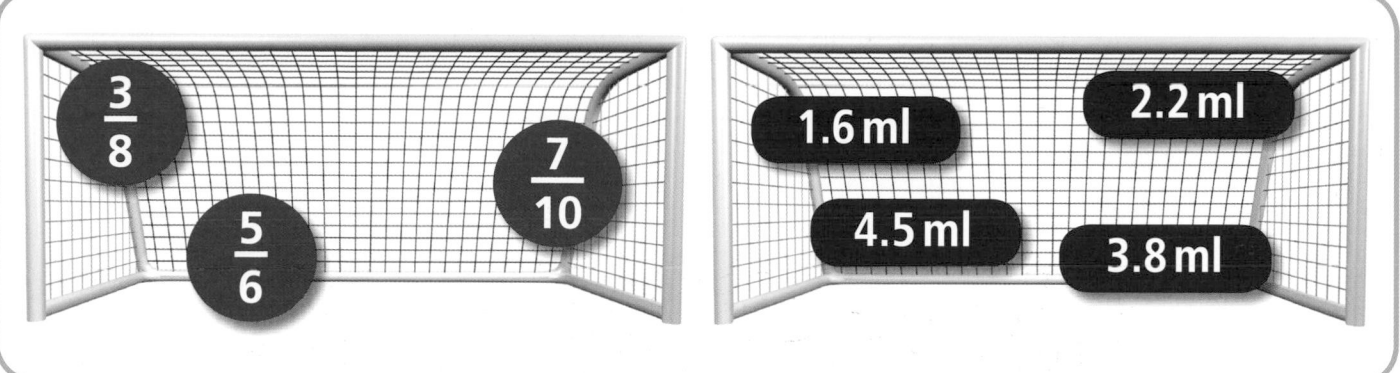

Kick-off

- Choose a fraction and a measurement from each goal.
- Use a calculator to find that fraction of the measurement.
- If you both agree on the answer, look below to see if one of the jars holds that amount. You may need to round the answer.
- Record the question and answer.
- Keep going until you have found all the amounts.

Manager's Message
To find the answer to $\frac{3}{8}$ of 1.6 on the calculator, key in 3 ÷ 8 × 1.6 =

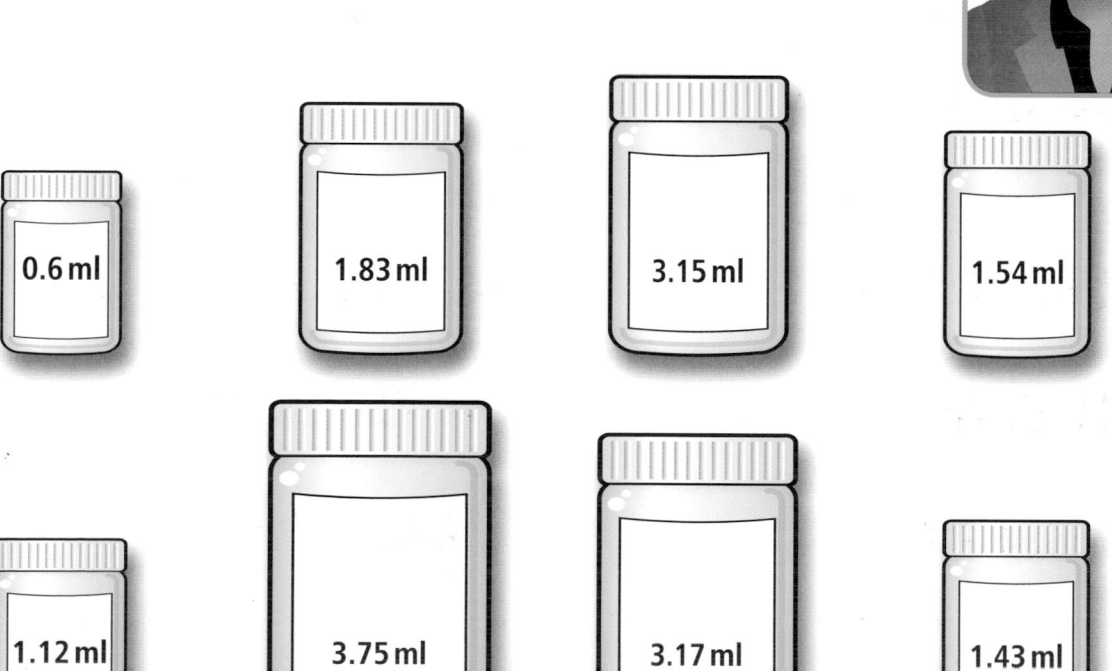

Shelby Town FC

Shelby Town FC,
24 Balcom Drive,
Shelby, Leeside

FAO All journalists and broadcasters

Welcome to another Premier League season at Manor Park. My name is Sandy Lane and I look after Press and Communications here at Shelby Town FC. I hope you got my note about our new press and broadcast facilities at home games.

We are now trying to provide you with all the statistical information you might need about the club. We have created special pages on the club website which you and our supporters will be able to access from today.

On these pages, you will find detailed rundowns on every Town match: results, teams, goals per match ratio, assists, passes, corners, tackles and so on. We will also summarise all those statistics so you get a picture of how the team is performing from week to week.

Please log on to the Shelby Town website to see the pages in action:

http://www.shelby.premiumtv/club/stats

Enjoy today's game!

Sandy Lane
Communications Officer, Shelby Town FC

Shelby Town

Sandy Lane
Communications Officer

Team Talk

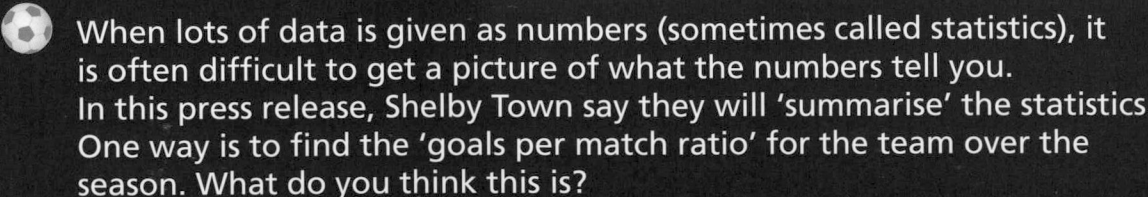

⚽ When lots of data is given as numbers (sometimes called statistics), it is often difficult to get a picture of what the numbers tell you. In this press release, Shelby Town say they will 'summarise' the statistics. One way is to find the 'goals per match ratio' for the team over the season. What do you think this is?

⚽ What does the word 'ratio' mean? Is a ratio of 3 goals in every 6 matches better, worse or the same as a ratio of 1 goal in every 2 matches?

Warm Up

▶ Use the vocabulary of ratio and proportion to describe the relationship between two numbers/quantities

1 For which of the matches below, is it true to say:

For every 1 goal Shelby Town scored, the other team scored 2.

Shelby Town results so far	
Shelby Town 1 : Tottenham Hotspur 2 ✓	Sunderland 2 : Shelby Town 2
Aston Villa 2 : Shelby Town 3	Shelby Town 2 : Man United 4
Bolton 3 : Shelby Town 1	Liverpool 6 : Shelby Town 3
Portsmouth 0 : Shelby Town 1	Shelby Town 1 : Manchester City 2

2 For each match, write what proportion of the goals Shelby Town scored. Give your answers as fractions.

Skills Practice

▶ Use the vocabulary of ratio and proportion to describe the relationship between two numbers/quantities

Work with a partner to solve these problems.

1

Shelby Town v Tottenham Hotspur	Sunderland v Shelby Town
6 corners : ___ corners	___ corners : 4 corners

In these two matches, it was true to say:

For every 2 corners Shelby Town was given, the other teams were given 1.

How many corners were the other teams given in these matches?

2

Shelby Town v Manchester City	Aston Villa v Shelby Town
6 corners : ___ corners	___ corners : 9 corners

In these two matches, it was true to say:

For every 3 corners Shelby Town was given, the other teams were given 1.

How many corners were the other teams given?

3

Shelby Town v Manchester United	Liverpool v Shelby Town
6 corners : ___ corners	___ corners : 9 corners

In these two matches, it was true to say:

For every 3 corners Shelby Town was given, the other teams were given 2.

How many corners were the other teams given?

4

Portsmouth v Shelby Town	Middlesbrough v Shelby Town
___ corners : 8 corners	___ corners : 4 corners

In these two matches, it was true to say:

For every 4 corners Shelby Town was given, the other teams were given 5.

How many corners were the other teams given?

Game On

The number of matches played and the number of goals scored for several clubs is given as a ratio.

Team	Matches : Goals	
Shelby Town	50	: 60
Newcastle	50	: 75
Chelsea	50	: 80
Arsenal	52	: 104
Bolton	55	: 66
Liverpool	40	: 64
Manchester United	55	: 110
Blackburn	48	: 72

1 Write each ratio in its simplest form by dividing both numbers in the ratio by the same number as many times as you can.

Shelby Town ÷ 10 ⌒ 50 : 60 ⌒ ÷ 10
5 : 6

2 Which clubs have the same matches to goals ratio?

3 Complete this sentence:
In every 5 matches, Shelby Town scored ___ goals.

4 Write a similar sentence for each of the other clubs.

> **Communications Officer's Message**
> It doesn't matter which numbers you divide by, as long as the answers are both whole numbers. Keep going until there are no more numbers that can divide into both.

The Big Match – Goal Per Match Ratio

Work with a partner. You will need a calculator each. Your job is to find out which teams have the highest goal per match ratio.

Kick-off

- Use the table from the Game On section.
- Both of you choose a club from the list.
- With a calculator, divide the number of goals by the number of matches for that club.
- This will give you the average number of goals per match.
- Record your answers following the example below.

	Matches	:	Goals
Shelby Town 60 ÷ 50	1	:	1.2

- Keep choosing pairs of clubs until you have found the number of goals per match for them all.
- Now put the clubs in order starting with the best goals per match ratio (the highest decimal).

Match day programme, Shelby Town v Newcastle United, August 29, Kick-off 3.00

Junior supporters' page

Shelby Town

Diane Eastham
Organiser, Junior Supporters Club

LATEST NEWS!
Well, the big news this week is that Shelby Town Junior Supporters' Club now has its own seven-a-side football team and we will be playing against other clubs during the rest of this season.

We hope that as many of you as possible will get the chance to play for the team.

WE NEED AN STJSC BADGE!
We all know what the Shelby Town club badge looks like. Now we need one for our own team, and it's up to you guys to design it!

We'd like the badge to remind people of the Shelby Town badge so we're looking for a colourful, symmetrical design but we also want it to be a bit different.

We'll pick the ten best entries and they will be judged by the boss, Mick Diamond. The winner will get two seats for a Town home game and a special prize awarded by Mick himself on the pitch before kick-off. Plus, your badge will go on our shirts!

Send your design, before October 31, to us here at Manor Park. You can either post it or email it to juniors@shelbytown.co.uk putting LOGO as the subject.

Get drawing and good luck!

Team Talk

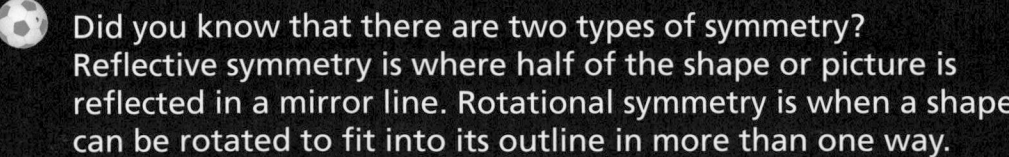

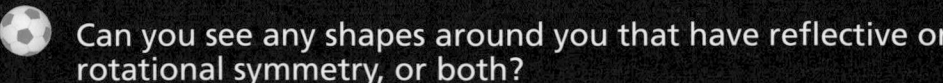

- Did you know that there are two types of symmetry? Reflective symmetry is where half of the shape or picture is reflected in a mirror line. Rotational symmetry is when a shape can be rotated to fit into its outline in more than one way.

- Can you see any shapes around you that have reflective or rotational symmetry, or both?

Warm Up

▶ Round 5-digit numbers to nearest 10, 100, 1000

The Junior Supporters' Club sells about 18 000 copies of its magazine each month.
Round these sales figures to the nearest 10, to the nearest 100 and to the nearest 1000

1   17 583   2   18 129   3   18 594   4   17 499

Skills Practice 1

▶ Complete patterns with up to two lines of symmetry

Fold a piece of A4 paper into quarters and place it on the paper outline below.
On your paper, sketch the reflections of each of the six logos in the dotted mirror lines.

Place your
paper on top
of this outline.

Skills Practice 2

▶ **Identify all the symmetries of 2D shapes**

1 With a partner, look at each letter.

STFC

Say whether each letter has reflective and/or rotational symmetry.

2 Write some other block capital letters and say whether each has reflective and/or rotational symmetry.

Game On

Match each logo with the correct description.

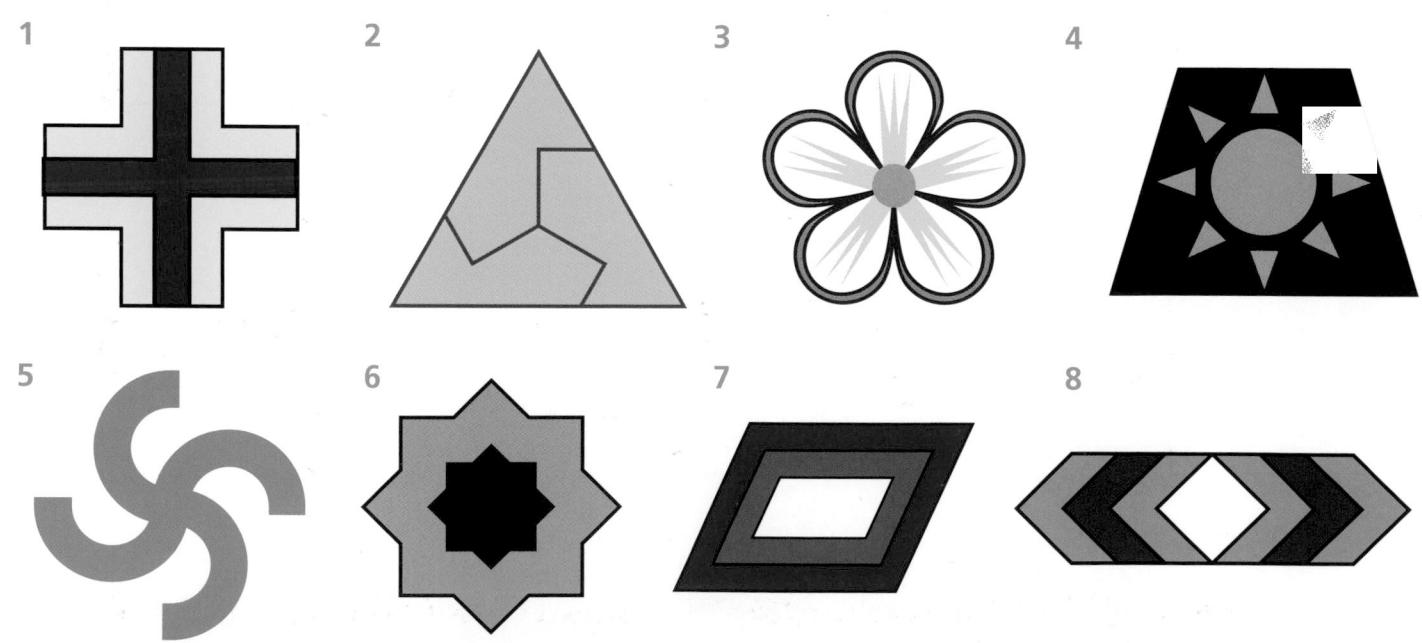

City's Supporters Club (CSC)
This logo has only
1 line of reflective symmetry and rotational symmetry of **order 1**.

Wanderers Youth Team (WYT)
This logo has
5 lines of reflective symmetry and rotational symmetry of **order 5**.

Town's Sports Association (TSA)
This logo has
no lines of reflective symmetry and rotational symmetry of **order 3**.

Rangers Reserves (RR)
This logo has
2 lines of reflective symmetry and rotational symmetry of **order 2**.

Athletic Juniors (AJ)
This logo has
4 lines of reflective symmetry and rotational symmetry of **order 4**.

United Fans Group (UFG)
This logo has
no lines of reflective symmetry and rotational symmetry of **order 2**.

Celtic Youth (CY)
This logo has
8 lines of reflective symmetry and rotational symmetry of **order 8**.

Orient Juniors (OJ)
This logo has
no lines of reflective symmetry and rotational symmetry of **order 4**.

The Big Match – STJSC Logo Competition

You will need coloured pencils.

Kick-off

- Design a logo for the Shelby Town Junior Supporters' Club.

STFC

Competition rules

- The design of the logo must fit inside an 8 cm x 8 cm square.

- It can be any shape or size but it must have rotational symmetry of order 4 and at least 2 lines of reflective symmetry.

- The colours must reflect the Shelby Town colours (red) but should use two other colours.

Shelby Town special occasion deals!

Why not surprise your friends and family with these amazing Premier League family treats?

Now with 36% off!

£40.00 **Package 1** **Original Special Treat**
- ✔ Pre-ordered message in match day programme
- ✔ Personal match escort
- ✔ Photograph with your favourite player

Max number of people 2

£60.00 **Package 2** **Signed Football**
- ✔ Pre-ordered message in match day programme
- ✔ Personal match escort
- ✔ Photograph with your chosen player
- ✔ Signed football presented to you by player

Max number of people 2

£90.00 **Package 3** **Family Package**
- ✔ Pre-ordered message in match day programme
- ✔ Personal match escort
- ✔ Photograph with your favourite player
- ✔ Group photograph with Shelby Town mascot
- ✔ Signed football presented to you by player

Max number of people 5

£130.00 **Package 4** **Signed Shirt**
- ✔ Pre-ordered message in match day programme
- ✔ Personal match escort
- ✔ Photograph with your favourite player
- ✔ Signed shirt presented to you by player

Max number of people 2

Team Talk

 These offers have a 36% discount. It means that 36% of the original price is taken off. What does 36% mean? If it has 36% taken off, what percentage of the original price do you pay?

 How could you work out 36% of a number using mental methods? Could you use 10% and 1% to help you? How do you work out 10% or 1% of a number? What could you do to find 30% or 5%?

Warm Up

▶ **Find percentages of numbers and quantities**

Use mental methods to answer these questions. Find 50% by halving, 25% by dividing by 4, 10% by dividing by 10 and 1% by dividing by 100.

1	50% of £52	**2**	25% of £48	**3**	10% of £32	**4**	1% of £250
5	50% of £77	**6**	25% of £56	**7**	10% of £117	**8**	1% of £76

Skills Practice 1

▶ **Find percentages of numbers and quantities**

1 Find 36% of each of the package prices. Do not use a calculator.

Package 1	Original Special Treat	Cost £40.00
Package 2	Signed Football	Cost £60.00
Package 3	Family Package	Cost £90.00
Package 4	Signed Shirt	Cost £130.00

2 Now work out the cost of each package in the sale.

Commercial Director's Message
Find 36% of a number by finding 25%, 10% and 1%, and adding the answers together.

Skills Practice 2

▶ **Find percentages of numbers and quantities**

Percentages of numbers can be calculated with or without a calculator.

Talk to a friend about whether it would be quicker to answer each question in your head, or use a calculator. Then work together to find the answers as quickly as you can.

1 50% of the squad of 24 players are under 25 years old. How many are under 25?

2 £3000 was raised for the Academy. 40% of this amount went towards new fitness equipment. How much was this?

3 67% of the 14 600 crowd were men. How many were men?

4 5% of the coaching staff are female. There are 20 members of staff. How many are female?

> **Commercial Director's Message**
> If using a calculator, remember
> that 42% means $\frac{42}{100}$ or 42 ÷ 100.
> So to find 42% of 85, key in
> 42 ÷ 100 x 85 =

Game On

One-day-only promotion – save 28% on the final cost of these offers

Town Suite hospitality offer	Jupiter Suite hospitality offer
✔ Cushioned seats	✔ Cushioned seats
✔ Pre-match three-course meal	✔ Pre-match one-course meal
✔ Drinks service to table	✔ Coffee and cakes at half-time
✔ Coffee and cakes at half-time	✔ Club host
✔ Club host and special guest appearance	✔ Match day programme
✔ Match day programme	
Match day £135 + VAT	**Match day £75 + VAT**

You may use a calculator for this activity. VAT is a tax added to many things and is usually 17.5% or $17\frac{1}{2}$%.

Find the final cost of the Town Suite and Jupiter Suite offers.

- First work out how much is the $17\frac{1}{2}$% VAT.
- Add this to the match day price.
- Find 28% of this total price.
- Subtract this answer to find the final cost.

Extra Time

 If a company decided to pay for 8 people to have the Jupiter Suite offer, how much would this cost? How much more would they have to pay to have the Town Suite offer?

The Big Match – Percentages

Play this game with a partner. You will need the Shelby cards, a dice and a calculator.

Kick-off

- Take turns. Roll the dice to give you a percentage.

 = 5%

- Then pick a Shelby Town card to tell you how many hundreds of pounds you have.

 = £1200

- The first player works out this percentage of the amount using mental methods.

  5% of £1200 = £60

- The second player works it out on the calculator to check the answer.
- If correct, the first player wins that amount of money.
- Take five goes each.
- The winner is the player with the most money in total at the end.
- Talk to your partner about how you worked out the answers each time.

Shelby Town

Brian Harris
Chief Scout

Memo

To: Jean Garde (JG), Malcolm Gibson (MG)
From: Brian Harris (BH)
Subject: Scouting staff trips – October/November

Jean and Malcolm,

I've got rough dates for you for the next month while I'm off scouting in Italy. Can you put them in your planners and let me have details of flight times, kick-offs, etc?

Jean Garde		**Malcom Gibson**	
Oct 21:	Lille	Oct 20:	Arsenal U-19
Oct 22:	Canne	Oct 21:	Boro U-17
Oct 24:	Fly Paris to Rome, meet BH	Oct 24:	Oldham
Oct 28:	Turin	Oct 25:	Wigan
Oct 30:	Fly Turin to Paris	Oct 28:	Fly Oslo
Oct 31:	Paris Saint-Germain	Oct 29–Nov 4:	Academy Tournament, Oslo
Nov 1:	Lens	Nov 5:	Fly Prague
Nov 3:	Fly Paris to Dallas	Nov 7:	Sparta
Nov 4–8:	International U-16 tournament, Dallas FC	Nov 8:	Slavia
Nov 9:	Fly Dallas to London	Nov 9:	Fly Manchester
Nov 10–13:	Shelby	Nov 10:	Bolton Reserves

Hope all that works. I'll let our match scouts know their dates in due course. Can you boys let me know what you need regarding flights, tickets, expenses, etc. and Jenny will arrange with the Club Secretary. See you here on Thursday.

Thanks!

Brian

Team Talk

⚽ There are many different ways of writing dates, such as 7th January 2009, 7-1-2009, 7 Jan 2009, 07/01/09. In what ways are these different? What do the numbers stand for?

⚽ How could you write the 9th October 2009 in different ways? Which do you think is the most commonly used way?

⚽ Which is the 7th month? The 4th month? The 11th month?

Warm Up

▶ **Read time on a 24-hour clock**

Write these times in words, saying whether it is a.m. or p.m.

1 11:55   **2** 14:25   **3** 16:40   **4** 07:05   **5** 21:10   **6** 23:35   **7** 00:50

Skills Practice 1

▶ **Use a calendar to calculate time intervals**

Brian Harris, Chief Scout, is going on a trip to Italy to see some potential new players. He will be visiting several clubs there to see them play. Here is his schedule.

October 2009

Mon	Tue	Wed	Thu	Fri	Sat	Sun
19	20	21	22	23	24 Fly to Rome	25 Roma match
26 Train to Genoa	27	28 Sampdoria match	29 Meet agent	30	31 Train to Milan	

November 2009

Mon	Tue	Wed	Thu	Fri	Sat	Sun
						1 AC Milan match
2	3 Meet agent	4 Inter Milan match	5	6 Fly home from Milan	7	8
9	10	11	12	13 Submit report	14	15

1 How many days will he spend in

  a) Rome?   **b)** Genoa?   **c)** Milan?

2 Write the date of each match in dd/mm/yy form.

3 On which days of the week is he meeting an agent?

4 How many nights will he spend in Italy in total?

Skills Practice 2

▶ **Read timetables and time using 24-hour clock notation**

On Brian's trip, he will travel from Rome (Roma) to Genoa (Genova). He looks at the train timetable to decide when to travel.

	Arr	Dep	Arr	Dep	Arr	Dep	Arr	Dep
Roma		07:45		09:57		11:57		17:57
Civitavecchia	08:23	08:25	10:32	10:34	12:32	12:34	18:32	18:34
Grosseto	09:20	09:22	11:27	11:30	13:27	13:29	19:27	19:29
Campiglia	09:54	09:55			13:57	13:58	19:57	19:58
Cecina	10:15	10:16					20:17	20:18
Livorno	10:40	10:42	12:40	12:42	14:40	14:42	20:42	20:44
Pisa	10:57	11:00	12:57	13:00	14:57	15:00	20:59	21:02
Viareggio	11:15	11:17			15:15	15:17	21:17	21:19
Massa	11:29	11:31	13:25	13:27			21:32	21:34
La Spezia	11:51	11:53	13:51	13:53	15:51	15:53	21:58	22:00
Sestri Levante					16:20	16:22	22:26	22:28
Chiavari	12:25	12:27	14:25	14:27			22:34	22:36
Genova	13:00		15:00		17:00		23:11	

Answer these questions, using a.m. or p.m. in your answers.

1 What time does the first train arrive at Genova?

2 What time does the second train depart from Roma?

3 What time does the fourth train depart from Roma?

4 What time does the third train arrive at Pisa?

5 What time does the second train depart from Pisa?

Game On

As he has some spare time, Brian decides to visit the Leaning Tower of Pisa on his trip. He would like to spend at least three hours there.

● What is his best option?

● Which trains should he catch?

● What time will he arrive in Genova?

The Big Match – Flight Times

Brian has received his flight details.

The arrival time in Rome and departure time in Milan are given in local Italian time. UK time is 1 hour behind Italian time.

London Gatwick (LGW) – Rome (FCO)

Flight 1　　Sat, October 24, 2009

Departure:	13:49	London Gatwick, North Terminal
Arrival:	18:07	Rome

　　　　　　　Fare type:　Economy

Milan (LIN) – London Gatwick (LGW)

Flight 2　　Fri, November 6, 2009

Departure:	18:17	Milan
Arrival:	20:08	London Gatwick, South Terminal

　　　　　　　Fare type:　Economy

Kick-off

Work with a partner to answer these questions.

1　What is the UK time when he

　a) arrives in Rome?　　　　　　b) leaves Milan?

2　How long is the flight

　a) to Rome?　　　　　　　　　b) from Milan?

3　He must be at the airport two hours before the departure time. What time must he arrive at

　a) Gatwick for the flight to Italy?　　b) Milan for the flight home?

Chief Scout's Message
Give your answers to Questions 1 and 3 in 12-hour clock, using a.m. or p.m.

Rob Mills (Presenter): *Thanks, Emma. More travel in half an hour on BBC Radio Leeside. Back to our phone-in now. We're talking about getting our kids to eat the right food and stay in shape. Here's a man who knows more than most about this. He's Niall Box, sports science supervisor for our own Shelby Town FC. Thanks for joining us, Niall.*

Niall Box: *Hi, Rob. I'll just put this bag of chips down. Only joking!*

Rob: *Very good, Niall. No chips at Manor Park these days, I bet.*

Niall: *Well, to be honest, Rob, chips now and again aren't the end of the world. We try and make sure the players get a well balanced diet. That means the right proportions of protein, carbs and everything else. Players are like fast cars – they need the right kind of fuel!*

Rob: *How do you work it all out?*

Niall: *Well, we have a nutrition expert who comes in every month and plans our menus. It all comes down to the percentages of the different food types in a player's diet. Get those right and you're fine.*

Rob: *You're making me feel hungry, Niall. Interesting stuff. Thanks. That's Niall Box from Shelby Town, live on Leeside.*

Team Talk

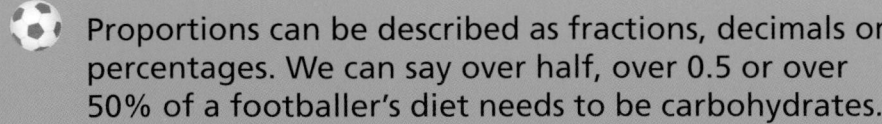 Proportions can be described as fractions, decimals or percentages. We can say over half, over 0.5 or over 50% of a footballer's diet needs to be carbohydrates.

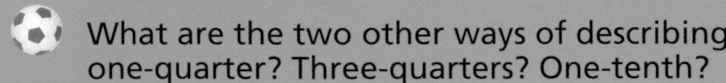 What are the two other ways of describing one-quarter? Three-quarters? One-tenth?

Warm Up

▶ **Find equivalent percentages, decimals and fractions**

Copy and complete these tables by filling in the missing fractions, decimals and percentages.

Percentage	Decimal	Fraction
50%		
		$\frac{1}{10}$
	0.2	
25%		
		$\frac{3}{4}$

Percentage	Decimal	Fraction
70%		
	0.3	
		$\frac{2}{5}$
	0.6	
		$\frac{1}{100}$

Skills Practice 1

▶ **Recognise approximate proportions of a whole and use fractions and percentages to describe and compare them**

You may use a calculator for these questions.

Major food groups	Recommended footballers' diet	Typical British diet
Carbohydrates	65%	$\frac{2}{5}$
Fats	$\frac{1}{5}$	45%
Proteins	15%	$\frac{3}{20}$

1 Copy the table, writing all the proportions as percentages.

2 a) If a footballer eats 4000 calories a day, how many calories should be carbohydrates?

   b) If a typical British person eats 4000 calories a day, how many calories are likely to be carbohydrates?

   c) How many more calories of carbohydrates does a footballer eat than a typical British person?

Fitness Coach's Message
To find 65% of 4000 on a calculator,
key in 65 ÷ 100 × 4000 =

3 a) If a footballer eats 4000 calories a day, how many calories should be fats?

b) If a typical British person eats 4000 calories a day, how many calories are likely to be fats?

c) How many fewer calories of fats does a footballer eat than a typical British person?

Skills Practice 2

▶ **Solve simple problems involving direct proportion by scaling quantities up or down**

Here are the prices of packs of healthy food items. Copy and complete five rows in each table to show how much it would cost for a larger number of the items.

1 1 energy drink costs £2

Bottles	Cost (£)
1	2
2	
3	
4	
5	

2 6 fruit bars costs £2

Bars	Cost (£)
6	2
12	
18	

3 5 oranges cost £3

Oranges	Cost (£)
5	3
10	
15	

4 4 tins of beans costs £3

Tins	Cost (£)
4	3

5 8 litres of milk costs £5

Litres	Cost (£)
8	5

6 10 apples cost £6

Apples	Cost (£)
10	6

Game On

Rewrite this recipe, changing it so that the ingredients are enough for 8 people.
You may use a calculator.

Creamy pea soup for 3 people
75 g butter
90 g peas (tinned or frozen, thawed)
150 ml chicken or vegetable stock
42 ml double cream
3 tbsp parsley, chopped

The Big Match - Food Proportions

Play this game with a partner. You will need a dice and a counter each.
Both players should write these amounts on a piece of paper.

£5   £6   £7   £8   £9   £10

Kick-off

- Place the counters on any starting position on the plate.

- Take turns to roll the dice and move your counter clockwise.

- Answer the question you land on. If it is one of your amounts, cross it off.

- Keep going until one player has crossed off all their amounts.

- The winner is the first to do this.

If 6 melons cost £4, how much do 9 cost?

If 2 apples cost £4, how much do 5 cost?

If 3 peppers cost £4, how much do 6 cost?

If 4 bananas cost £6, how much do 6 cost?

If 6 sprouts cost £2 how much do 18 cost?

If 3 peaches cost £4.20, how much do 5 cost?

If 5 beetroots cost £4, how much do 10 cost?

If 5 plums cost £3, how much do 10 cost?

If 4 pears cost £1, how much do 20 cost?

If 2 carrots cost £3, how much do 6 cost?

If 3 tomatoes cost £3.60, how much do 5 cost?

If 4 oranges cost £6, how much do 2 cost?

WIN WITH SHELBY TOWN AT MANOR PARK

Take your business into the Premier League with Town!

Why not take advantage of the capacity crowds and TV and media coverage that have come with Town hitting the big time?

We're offering match-by-match and season-long deals for businesses large and small. Hook your business up to our success story and reach 30 000 people or more every Manor Park match day.

★ **MATCH BALL SPONSORSHIP £500** ★
★ **KIT SPONSORSHIP £350** ★
★ **VIDEO SCREEN CLIPS FROM £80** ★
★ **PERIMETER BOARDS FROM £50** ★
★ **PROGRAMME ADVERTISING FROM £35** ★
★ **WEBSITE PROMOTIONS FROM £30** ★
★ **AND MUCH MORE!!!** ★

**We'll make it work for your business,
however big or small your budget.**

Call the Sales Team today or email us: sales@shelbytown.co.uk

Team Talk

⚽ Advertising charges depend on the length of the advert. Smaller or shorter adverts cost less than larger or longer ones. Often a formula is given so that people can work out how much an advert would cost. What is a formula? What might it look like and how would you use it?

⚽ If an advert costs £2 per letter plus a £10 charge, what might a formula for the cost look like?

Warm Up

▶ Find missing numbers in calculations

1 27 + __ = 100	2 45 − __ = 6	3 7 × __ = 28	4 24 ÷ __ = 8
5 __ + 18 = 100	6 __ − 22 = 31	7 __ × 9 = 45	8 __ ÷ 5 = 20

Skills Practice 1

▶ Construct and use simple expressions and formulae in words then symbols

Here are some of the club advertising promotions for businesses.

Advertise on the Shelby Town video screen!
Only £70 plus £10 for each second of your advert

Sponsor a Shelby Town player! Get your logo on his shirt!
Only £500 plus £17 per month

Put an advert in the Shelby Town monthly magazine – Extra Time!
Only £35 plus 50p for each letter of your advert

The cost of advertising on the video screen (the first advert) can be written using symbols, like this

the cost (in pounds)   the number of seconds

$$c = 70 + 10n$$

> **Manager's Message**
> Use **n** to stand for the number of months or the number of letters in the advert.

Write the cost in pounds, **c**, for the other two promotions, using symbols.

Skills Practice 2

▶ **Construct and use simple expressions and formulae in words then symbols**

1 Use this formula to help you find the cost of these video screen adverts, where *n* is the number of seconds.

$$c = 70 + 10n$$

What is the cost in pounds, *c*, for a

a) 5 second advert?   b) 8 second advert?   c) 13 second advert?

d) 30 second advert?   e) 1 minute advert?   f) 2 minute advert?

2 Use this formula to help you find the cost of sponsoring a player, where *n* is the number of months of sponsorship.

$$c = 500 + 17n$$

What is the cost in pounds, *c*, for sponsoring the player for

a) 2 months?   b) 10 months?   c) 1 year?

3 Use this formula to help you find the cost of an advert in Extra Time magazine, where *n* is the number of letters of the advert.

$$c = 35 + 0.5n$$

What is the cost in pounds, *c*, for an advert with

a) 10 letters?   b) 100 letters?   c) 50 letters?

Game On

Find the total cost of these promotions.

25 second advert on the video screen

3 year sponsorship of player

This advert in Extra Time magazine

Seymour Films

DVD rental
Simply the best

The Big Match - Cost It!

Play this game with a partner. You will need the Shelby Town cards from 1 to 10, a dice and a counter each.

Kick-off

- Place the counters on any starting position on the track.
- Take turns to roll the dice and move your counter clockwise.
- When you land, pick a Shelby Town card to give you the value of **n**.
- Find the value of **s**. This is your score.
- Take five turns each and find your total scores.
- The winner is the player with the highest score.

$s = 5 + 3n$	$s = 2 + 7n$	$s = 4 + 3n$	$s = 8 + 5n$
$s = 3 + 6n$			$s = 2 + n$
$s = 7 + 5n$			$s = 4 + 7n$
$s = 6 + 6n$			$s = 3 + 5n$
$s = 5 + 2n$			$s = 9 + 3n$
$s = 8 + 7n$	$s = 6 + 9n$	$s = 5 + n$	$s = 4 + 2n$

s = your score

n = the number on the dice

!!!! CALLING ALL TOWN FANS !!!!

If you only buy one Christmas present this year, make sure it's this one!

The Shelby Town Premier League Pen is the perfect stocking filler. It costs just £5, and hidden inside could be a season ticket, signed match ball or one of dozens of other great mystery prizes! You won't know what you've won until you open it on Xmas Day! One in every ten pens has a voucher for a special prize inside the lid.

The ST Pens are promoted by the ST Lottery Fund: all the profits will help fund the work of Derek Hardaker and his team at the Shelby Town Academy.

Prizes include

★ 09/10 STFC season ticket

★ STFC match tickets

★ signed STFC shirts and balls

★ match programmes

★ catering vouchers

and many more!!!!

Shelby Town Pens are available now, from the club shop, newsagents and outlets all over Shelby. Buy one now and help bring on the stars of the future at Manor Park!

Team Talk

It says that 1 in every 10 pens has a prize inside the lid.
Does this mean you have a good chance of winning a prize?
Is it likely or unlikely that you will win if you buy 1 pen?

What does probability mean?
What is the probability of winning a prize in the competition?
If you bought 10 pens, would you be certain to win a prize?

Warm Up

▶ **Describe the occurrence of familiar events using the language of chance or likelihood**

We use the words below when describing the probability of something, or how likely it is to happen.

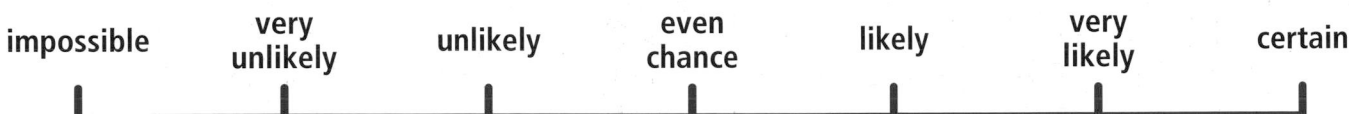

impossible   very unlikely   unlikely   even chance   likely   very likely   certain

Talk to a partner. Decide on a word to describe the probability of each of these events.

1   I will roll the number 6 on a normal dice.

2   It will rain in London in February.

3   I will pick a red card from a pack of cards.

4   The day after Saturday is Sunday.

Skills Practice 1

▶ **Understand and use the probability scale from 0 to 1; find and justify probabilities based on equally likely outcomes in simple contexts**

1 One of these players is picked at random. What is the likelihood he will be wearing

a) an odd number?   b) a multiple of 3?   c) a number greater than 6?

d) a 9?   e) a number greater than 5?   f) a number greater than 0?

g) a 12?   h) a prime number?   i) a factor of 12?

2 Now mark the probabilities you have given on a probability scale like this one, split into 10 equal parts.

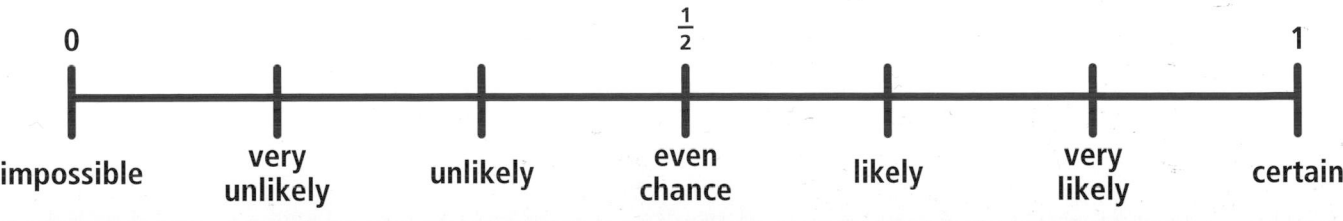

0                                    $\frac{1}{2}$ 1

impossible   very unlikely   unlikely   even chance   likely   very likely   certain

Skills Practice 2

▶ **Understand and use the probability scale from 0 to 1; find and justify probabilities based on equally likely outcomes in simple contexts**

The promotions team has come up with a 'golden ticket' idea where some tickets will be hidden inside special pens. It is discussing how many tickets to hide and how many pens to sell.

1 Write the probability, as a fraction in its simplest form, of winning a golden ticket if there are

a) 10 golden tickets inside 50 pens   b) 10 golden tickets inside 100 pens

c) 5 golden tickets inside 100 pens   d) 1 golden ticket inside 500 pens

e) 30 golden tickets inside 3000 pens   f) 5 golden tickets inside 2500 pens

g) 1 golden ticket inside 2000 pens   h) 4 golden tickets inside 1000 pens

2 Are any probabilities in Question 1 the same? Where would the probabilities be marked on a probability scale? Talk to your partner about these questions.

3 The promotions team decide that the probability should be $\frac{1}{250}$. They want to sell 2000 pens. How many golden tickets should they hide?

Game On

The promotions team also decide to sell lottery tickets at each home match. Every winner receives a free burger at one of the snack bars.

Rules

Tickets are 50p.

Each ticket shows a number between 2 and 12.

At half time, two large dice are rolled on the pitch and the two numbers are added together.

Anyone with that total on their ticket can collect a free burger.

RAFFLE 7   RAFFLE 2   RAFFLE 8   5   10

1 Which ticket number or numbers do you think it is best to have? Which totals are most likely to occur? Talk to a partner and try to find out why.

2 Write all the possible rolls of two dice and their totals.

3 What is the probability of getting these totals?

a) 2   b) 5   c) 6   d) 7   e) 10   f) 12

The Big Match – Probability Prizes

Work with a partner. You will need the Shelby Town cards, marked from 1 to 24. Shuffle the cards and spread them face down on the table.

Kick-off

- Choose one of the prize rules from the grid below.

- Work out the probability of winning a prize with this rule, giving your answer as a fraction.

- Then pick a card at random to see if you win the prize.

- Replace the card and shuffle the pack.

- Continue in this way, recording your probabilities until you have completed all nine rules.

Rule 1 Win a prize if the number is a multiple of 3	**Rule 2** Win a prize if the number is less than 11	**Rule 3** Win a prize if the number is more than 20
Rule 4 Win a prize if the number is a multiple of 5	**Rule 5** Win a prize if the number is odd	**Rule 6** Win a prize if the number is a square number
Rule 7 Win a prize if the number is a prime number	**Rule 8** Win a prize if the number is a factor of 24	**Rule 9** Win a prize if the number is between 15 and 20 (inclusive)

Extra Time

- If picking a card from the set of numbers 1 to 24 at random, with which rule are you most likely to win?

- If picking a card from the set of numbers 1 to 24 at random, with which rule are you least likely to win?

- Draw a probability scale and mark on the probabilities for each rule.

NOW SPORTS
LIVE

Dougie Ball (Studio Presenter): Sky Super Sunday comes live from Manor Park this afternoon. Shelby Town versus Fulham kicks off at 4 p.m. Already there for us is commentator Martin Tyler.

Martin Tyler: Thanks Dougie. Cold February afternoon in Shelby but the sun's shining and I have to say the playing surface here is looking marvellous. The man to thank for that is Town's head groundsman, Cliff Warriner.

Cliff Warriner: Hello Martin.

Martin: You're the youngest groundsman in the Premier League, Cliff, so you may not remember the days when every pitch, this time of year, looked like a muddy beach! What's the secret?

Cliff: Well, we don't just mow the area and hope for the best these days, Martin! Every summer, every square inch of the surface is re-seeded. We split the pitch up into yard-wide strips and really work on each one as if it's a little lawn. We know to the last drop how many gallons we need to put on the grass and when.

Martin: Sounds very scientific, Cliff.

Cliff: I suppose it is. In the old days, groundsmen did their best but they just splashed gallons of water on the grass when it was dry and covered it an inch deep in sand when it got soft. Now, Mr Diamond tells us exactly what he wants, how many centimetres of growth he wants on the grass for the game and we do the rest.

Martin: Well, it'll be perfect for Town and Fulham later today. I'm going to have a chat with Cliff about sorting out my back garden now! So it's back to you in the studio, Dougie.

Team Talk

⚽ What does the word 'area' mean? Can you think of different areas in your school or house? How do we measure area? What is the difference between area and perimeter?

⚽ Do you know the approximate relationships between gallons and litres, yards and metres and inches and centimetres?

Warm Up

▶ **Select and use standard metric units of measure and convert between units using decimals**

Copy and complete these.

> **Head Groundsman's Message**
> There are 10 mm in 1 cm, 100 cm in 1 m, 1000 m in 1 km, 1000 g in 1 kg and 1000 ml in 1 litre.

1 48 cm = _____ mm

2 137 cm = _____ m

3 540 mm = _____ cm

4 125 mm = _____ cm

5 2000 m = _____ km

6 10 000 m = _____ km

7 500 m = _____ km

8 5000 g = _____ kg

Skills Practice

▶ **Use the formula for the area of a rectangle**
▶ **Solve problems by measuring, estimating and calculating**

Use a calculator to help you find the area inside each dotted outline.

1

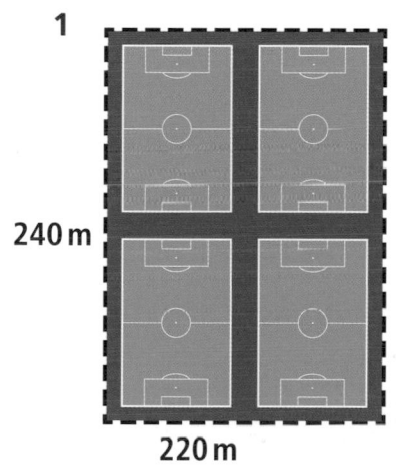

240 m

220 m

2

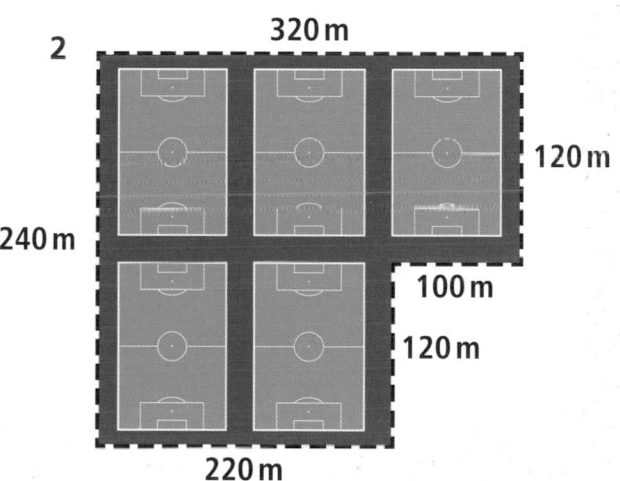

320 m

120 m

240 m

100 m

120 m

220 m

3

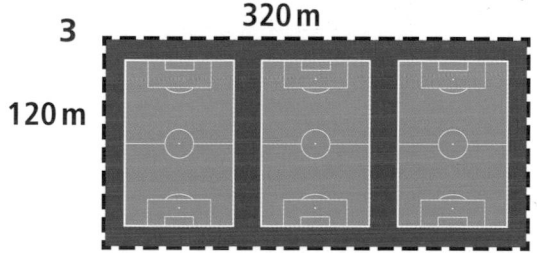

320 m

120 m

4

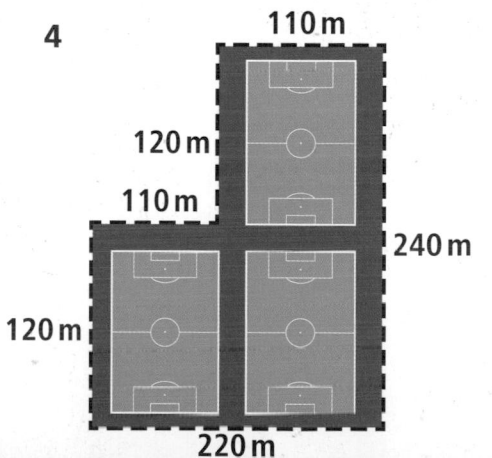

110 m

120 m

110 m

240 m

120 m

120 m

220 m

Game On

The groundsman wants to re-seed some of the pitches at the training ground. The area that he wants to re-seed is marked with a dotted line.

Work with a friend to solve these problems. You may use a calculator.

1 Work out the missing numbers on the diagram.

2 Calculate the area of the ground inside the dotted line, giving your answer in square metres.

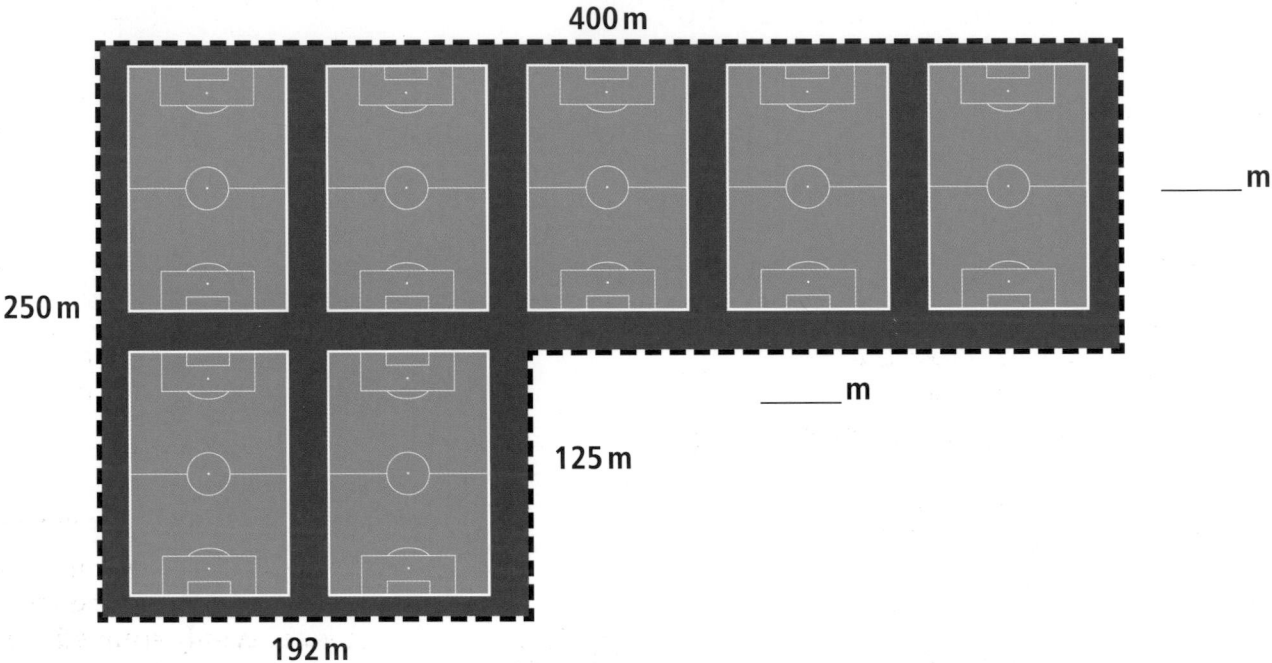

3 To establish good even grass, he must use 50 g of grass seed per metre square.

  a) How many grams of grass seed will he need?

  b) How many kilograms is this?

  c) If grass seed costs £3 per kilogram, how much will all the seed cost?

4 After the grass is established, he will put on fertiliser. He must use 24 g of fertiliser per metre square.

  a) How many grams of fertiliser will he need?

  b) How many kilograms is this?

  c) If fertiliser costs £2.50 per kilogram, how much will all the fertiliser cost?

5 What will the total cost be for the grass seed and the fertiliser?

The Big Match - Watering Systems

Shelby Town is installing sprinkler systems to water the pitches. The pop-up sprinklers spray water as shown in the diagram.

The watering system will spray 240 litres per minute across one football pitch.

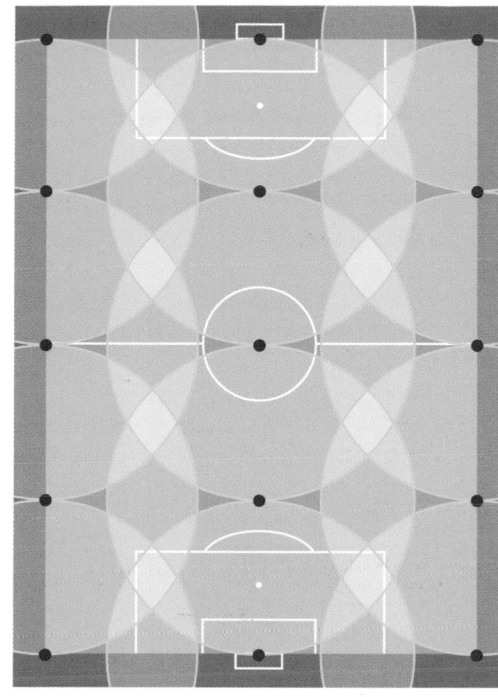

Kick-off

- Work with a partner to answer each of these questions from the ground staff.
- You may use a calculator.

> How much water will be sprayed across the pitch in 1 hour?

> If 1 gallon is about 4.5 litres, how many gallons are sprayed per hour?

> How many litres of water are sprayed each second?

> If the football pitch has an area of 6400 m², and the water is evenly sprayed, how much water will fall on each square metre in one hour?

> How many millilitres is this?

> **Groundsman's Message**
> Remember there are 60 seconds in a minute and 60 minutes in one hour.

Midlands Business Life

Underdogs Cash In On Big Time

By Our Staff Reporter

It's the kind of story football fans love – a little club taking its chance on the big stage in the Premier League. Shelby Town, after years in the lower divisions, reached the Premier League last season. Careful management on and off the pitch were behind Town's rise from obscurity. The same principles enabled them to cash in after a first-ever season in the top flight.

Figures released by the club yesterday show a massive jump in profits, thanks to the extra income generated from Premier League status.

Jane Saunders is the CEO at Town's 25 000 capacity ground. 'We're all delighted,' she said yesterday. 'This is a tribute to the hard work of Mr Carstairs, our chairman, the manager, Mick Diamond, and all the players. Our income from ticket sales has been very strong for several years now but income from other sectors – slices of the football pie, if you like – have rocketed.'

'We've been able to bank our share of television revenues, of course. But we've also seen income from sponsorship and commercial activities increase.'

Much of Town's extra income will go on wages and transfer fees, of course. The trick now will be for them to stay in the Premier League. Watch this space!

Team Talk

 Proportions of a whole can be shown as pie charts. If 33.3% of Shelby's income comes from match day income (sales of tickets, food, drink and car park charges, etc.), what fraction of the whole pie chart is this?

 How many degrees are in a full turn? What will be the angle at the centre of the pie chart for the 'match day' sector?

Warm Up

▶ **Find factors of numbers to 100**

Write all the factors of

1 12   **2** 16   **3** 30   **4** 36   **5** 50   **6** 100

Skills Practice 1

▶ **Interpret pie charts**

▶ **Recognise approximate proportions of a whole and use fractions and percentages to describe and compare them, for example when interpreting pie charts**

This pie chart shows the proportions of income (sometimes called turnover) that come from different parts of Shelby Town club. The total income at the club in 2008 was 36 million pounds (£36m).

Pie chart to show the proportions of £36m income at Shelby Town in 2008

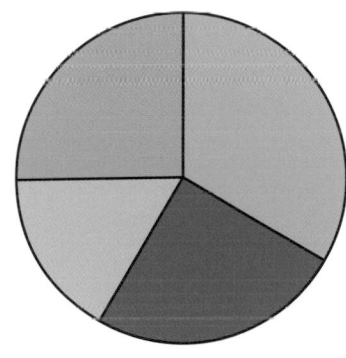

◯ **Match day** (sales at Manor Park such as tickets, food, drink, car park charges, etc.)

⬤ **Sponsorship** (including hospitality packages)

◯ **Commercial** (Shelby Town shop sales)

◯ **Broadcast** (payments for playing matches on TV and radio)

1 Estimate what fraction of the Shelby Town income came from

    a) match day sales   **b)** sponsorship   **c)** commercial sales   **d)** broadcast

2 Write the fractions from your answers to Question 1 as percentages.

3 Estimate how many million pounds came from

    a) match day sales   **b)** sponsorship   **c)** commercial sales   **d)** broadcast

Skills Practice 2

▶ **Interpret pie charts**

These pie charts show the proportions of income for Shelby Town for 2007 and 2008.

In 2007, Shelby Town's income was **£24m**.   In 2008, it was **£36m**.

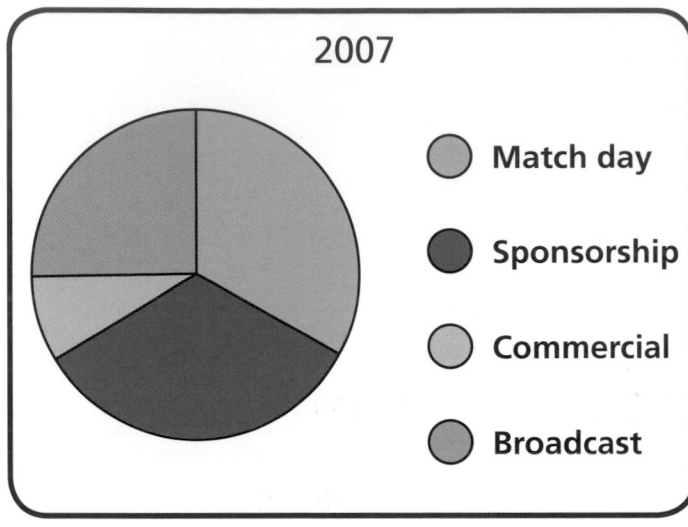

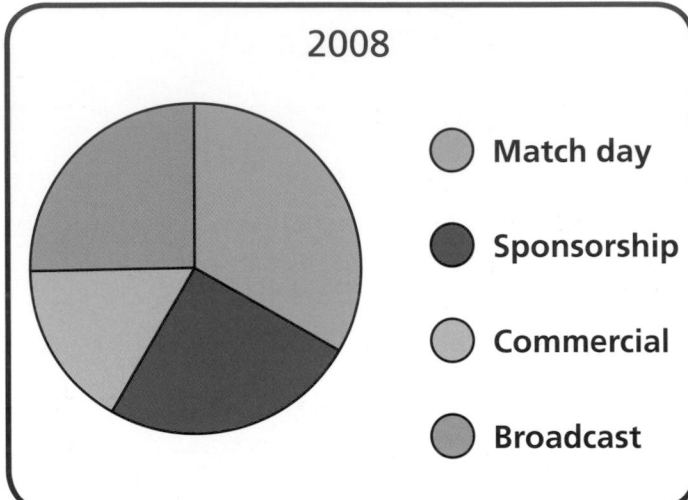

1 For 2007, estimate how many million pounds came from

a) match day sales   **b)** sponsorship   **c)** commercial sales   **d)** broadcast

Game On

1 Use your answers to Skills Practice 1 and 2 to help you say whether each statement is true or false.

a) In 2007, Shelby Town received one-third of its income from sponsorship.

b) In 2008, Shelby Town received one-third of its income from sponsorship.

c) Shelby Town received more money from sponsorship in 2007 than in 2008.

d) One-quarter of Shelby Town's income in both years was from broadcasting.

e) In 2008, £9m came from broadcasting. In 2007, only £6m came from broadcasting.

f) Shelby Town had the same income for match day sales in both years.

2 Write three more true statements of your own.

Chief Executive's Message
Remember that the two pie charts represent different amounts. For example, $\frac{1}{4}$ of the first pie chart is not worth the same as $\frac{1}{4}$ of the second pie chart.

The Big Match – Roll Up

Work with a partner.

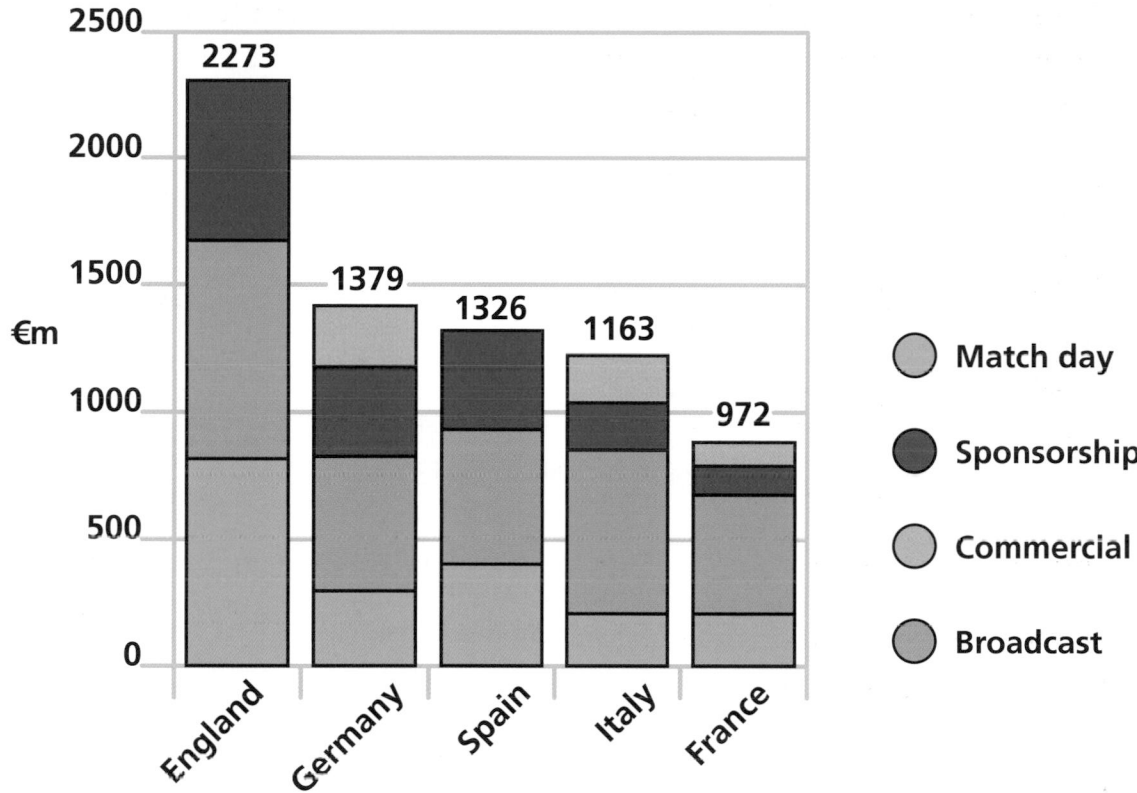

How the European leagues make their money

Legend:
- Match day
- Sponsorship
- Commercial
- Broadcast

Kick-off

- Look at this graph.
- With your partner, discuss what it shows.
- It might help you to copy and complete a table like this, making estimates from the graph.

	England	Germany	Spain	Italy	France
Match day	£800m				
Broadcast					
Sponsorship					
Commercial					

- Together, write at least five statements about the differences between the incomes of the top league clubs in European countries, and where those incomes are received from.
- Use whole numbers and fractions in your statements.

Match day programme Shelby Town v Arsenal, April 13, Kick-off 4.00

April 13

The Diamond vision

Welcome to Manor Park for the last but one home game of what's been a great season for the club. I have to pinch myself sometimes – Shelby Town versus Arsenal, today. Hope Arsene Wenger enjoys his visit to Manor Park. Hope you will, too.

Just thought I'd let you know about plans for pre-season. We have been invited to the Far East for games in Hong Kong, China and a mini-tournament in Seoul in South Korea. This is great news for the club – a chance to take the Shelby Town message to the other side of the world.

We will travel across several time zones, so we'll have to monitor the players for the effects of jetlag. Shanghai, our first stop, is 8 hours ahead of UK time, for example!

It's a world game now, though, and I often find myself having to work out different time zones anyway. If a game I want to see from a South American league is on TV, I have to work out how many hours behind us they are to be able to set the DVD player for the right time!

Anyway, all that's for July. Today, it's about getting the better of the Gunners. Look at their dressing room – all internationals and a few different time zones when it comes to the countries they represent, too! Enjoy the match.

Up the Town!

Mick Diamond

Team Talk

 Why do different countries around the world have different times?

 Why is it 12 o'clock in London and 7 o'clock in New York?

Warm Up

▶ **Order positive and negative integers and decimals**

Put these integers in order, starting with the smallest.

1 7, 3, -4, -8, -1, 0, 8   **2** -1, -4, -7, 3, -2, 4, 7

3 -5, -10, -9, -15, 3, 1.5, -12   **4** -12, -6, 0.5, -9, 0.75, 9, -1

Skills Practice 1

▶ **Use positive and negative numbers in context and knowledge of addition and subtraction facts**

Will Johnson, the travel manager, is telephoning clubs in other countries to set up a pre-season tour. He looks at the World Time Zones map to find out what time it is in these other countries.

World time zone map

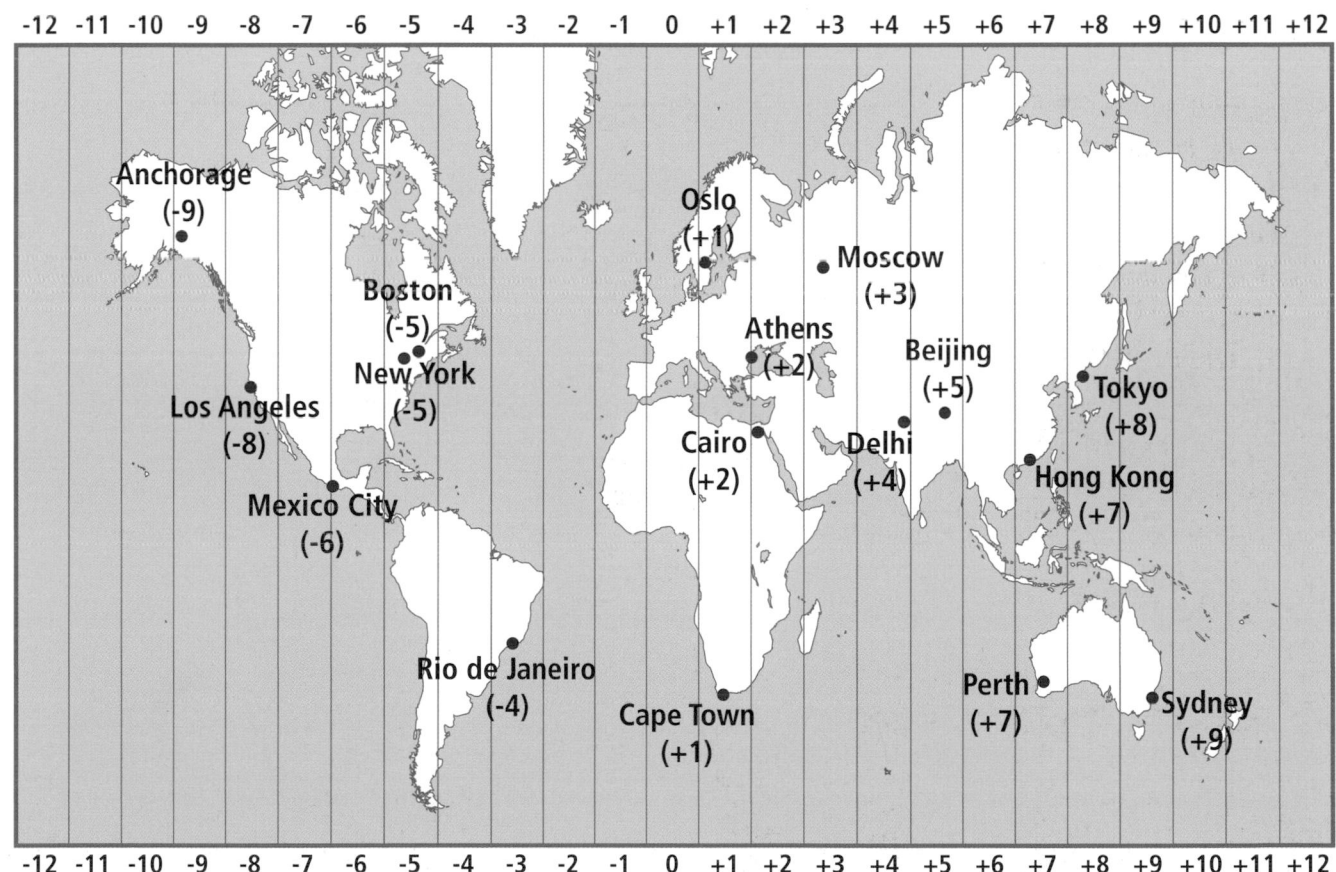

It is 12:00 noon in Shelby.
Use the 24-hour clock to write what time it is in

1 Mexico City	**2** Athens	**3** Rio de Janeiro	**4** Hong Kong
5 Anchorage	**6** Los Angeles	**7** Sydney	**8** Boston

Skills Practice 2

▶ **Find the difference between a positive and a negative integer, or two negative integers, in context**

Will is also finding out about the temperatures in each place because he doesn't want the team to go from one place to another and experience too large a temperature change.

What is the difference between these pairs of temperatures?

1 Hong Kong 22°C and Moscow -7°C

2 Anchorage -5°C and Beijing 3°C

3 New York 14°C and Mexico City 16°C

4 Oslo -1°C and Moscow -7°C

5 Sydney 20°C and Oslo -1°C

6 Los Angeles 14°C and Anchorage -5°C

7 Beijing 3°C and Oslo -1°C

8 Beijing 3°C and Moscow -7°C

9 Anchorage -5°C and Moscow -7°C

10 Oslo -1°C and Anchorage -5°C

Game On

When looking on the internet for information, Will finds this chart.

Location	Highest recorded temperature (°C)	Lowest recorded temperature (°C)	Height above sea level (m)
Cape Town, South Africa	41	-2.1	6
Seville, Spain	50	-10	10
Cairo, Egypt	45	1	64
Death Valley, USA	57.6	-9.4	-86
Dead Sea (West Bank)	51.2	-12	-418
Shanghai, China	40.2	-12.1	4
Kathmandu, Nepal	37.2	-3.5	1336
Thessaloniki, Greece	43.2	-14	2
Paris, France	40.4	-23.9	35
Vostok, Antarctica	-13.6	-89.2	3488
Perth, Australia	46.2	-0.7	15
London, England	38.1	-18.8	43

Work with a partner. Choose some of the questions from the grid on the next page to investigate the information in the table. Write facts about the information to present to the rest of the group.

Which place has the lowest recorded temperature?	Which place has the highest recorded temperature?	Which two places are below sea level (0 m)?	Find two places that have sea levels with a difference of 96 m.	Find two places with a highest temperature difference of 54°C.
Which place has never had temperatures below freezing (0°C)?	Which place has a lowest temperature between 0°C and -1°C?	What is the difference between the lowest temperatures of Cairo and Paris?	Find two places that have sea levels with a difference of 453 m.	What is the difference between the lowest temperatures of Cape Town and Shanghai?

The Big Match – Negativity

Play this game with a friend. You will need a counter and the Shelby Town cards.

Draw a large number line with numbers from -25 to 25.
-25 and 25 are the goals of a football pitch. The centre spot is at zero.

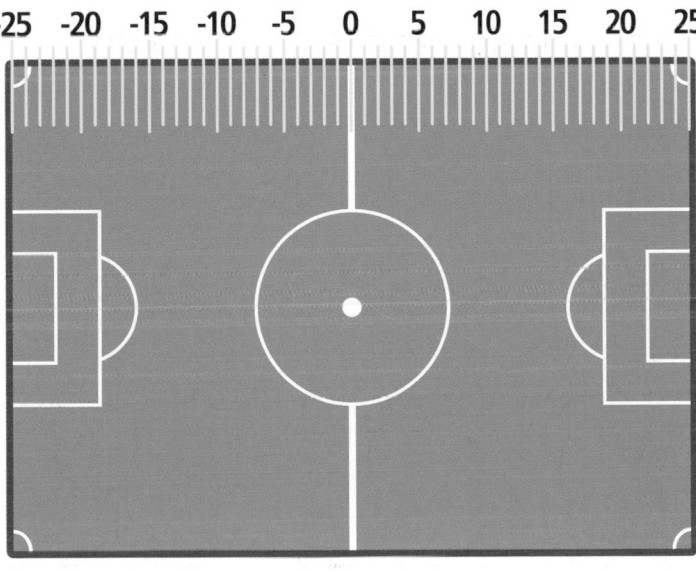

Kick-off

- Place the counter at zero.
- Take turns to pick a Shelby Town card and move the counter towards your goal.
- One player moves to the left towards -25 and the other moves to the right towards 25.
- As each turn is taken, record where the counter was and where it ended up as shown in the example.

    -5 and 9. Difference of 14

    The difference will always be the number of the Shelby Town card picked.

- If you reach 25 or -25, that player scores a goal.
- The winner is the player with the most goals at the end.

https://www.shelby.premiumtv.co.uk/rater

Most Visited ▾   Getting Started   Latest Headlines ﹚

Shelby Town FC
SHELBY TOWN PLAYER RATER

Home

News

Manager's page

Fixtures

Match reports

Player rater

Online shop

Contact us

Season tickets still available at discount when you buy online!

SQUAD   MATCH   TEAM   FANS

1 JENKS   9 ODEGBAME

2 JONES   10 ALLENBY

3 BALL   11 DUNNE

4 SEFTON   12 DOVE

SUBS BENCH

Here's your chance to rate Town's players from week to week, and to keep track of who's having a good season and who still has work to do.

How to play

1 Click MATCH to choose the game you want to mark the players' performances in.

2 Click TEAM to make the team for that game (plus subs) appear.
  You can then award each player between 1 and 10 out of 10.

3 Click FANS to see what other people have made of the performance with our average marks out of ten. Follow the link to chart each player's performances over the season.

Done

Team Talk

 What does the word 'average' mean?

Do you know any types of average?
What are the differences between these averages?

Warm Up

▶ Find the range of a set of numbers

Shelby Town fans have been marking the players out of 10 for their performance after a Saturday afternoon match. So far, 11 fans have rated the players.

Find the **range** for each player by subtracting the lowest rating from the highest rating.

Peter Jenks	6	7	5	6	7	4	6	5	6	7	5
Peter Ball	8	6	8	8	4	7	8	6	7	3	6
Al Sefton	7	6	7	6	7	6	6	6	7	6	7
Dave Morgan	9	7	8	9	10	6	8	9	9	9	9
Timmo Hannesen	4	5	7	4	6	7	5	6	4	7	5
Danny Smith	9	8	9	9	9	9	8	9	8	8	8
Stuart Dolan	10	10	9	10	10	9	9	8	10	2	10
Dotun Odegbame	8	7	8	6	9	7	4	8	9	8	9
Tom Allenby	5	6	7	5	6	7	8	5	5	6	7
Pierre Jean Vert	3	4	3	5	2	4	5	4	5	4	4
Adrian Emilio	8	9	8	9	9	9	10	7	10	9	8

Skills Practice 1

▶ Describe and interpret results and solutions to problems using the mode, median and mean

Find the mode, median and mean of each player's ratings.
Use the information below to help you.

● To find the **mode**, look for the most popular, or frequent, value or values in the list.

    4, 3, 7, 8, 3   Most frequent value   The **mode** is **3**

● To find the **median**, put all the scores in order and then find the middle value. If there are two middle values, then the median is the number halfway between them.

    3, 3, 4, 7, 8   Middle value   The **median** is **4**

● To find the **mean**, find the total of all the scores then divide this by the number of scores.

    4 + 3 + 7 + 8 + 3 = 25   25 ÷ 5 = 5   The **mean** is **5**

Skills Practice 2

▶ **Construct and interpret frequency diagrams and bar charts with grouped data**

The fans continue to post their ratings on the Shelby Town website. The mean average of all the fans ratings for the Saturday match is given for each player.

Peter Jenks	6.8
Dave Morgan	8.9
Stuart Dolan	9.1
Pierre Jean Vert	4.0

Peter Ball	7.2
Timmo Hannesen	6.1
Dotun Odegbame	7.8
Adrian Emilio	8.9

Al Sefton	6.5
Danny Smith	8.8
Tom Allenby	6.7

1 Copy and complete this table to show the team's ratings.

Mean rating (out of 10)	Frequency
0 – 1.9	
2 – 3.9	
4 – 5.9	
6 – 7.9	
8 – 9.9	

2 Draw a frequency diagram (bar chart) for this information.

Game On

This frequency diagram shows how the same players were rated for the Wednesday night match.

Talk to a partner about these questions.

1 Which players were rated worse on Wednesday than on Saturday?

2 How can you be sure?

3 Could any of the players have been rated better on Wednesday than on Saturday?

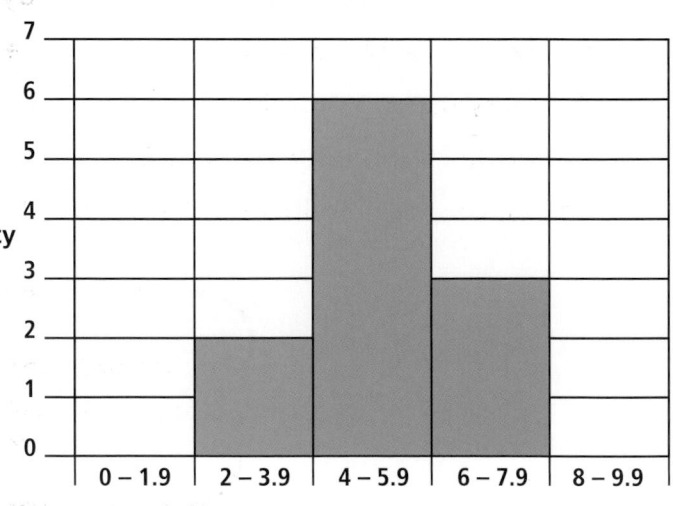

The Big Match – Mean Scores

Play this game with a partner. You will need the Shelby Town cards and a calculator.

Kick-off

- Shuffle the cards and spread them face down on the table.
- Round 1: both players should pick 4 cards.

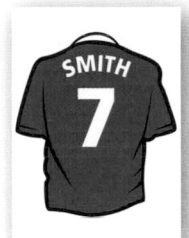 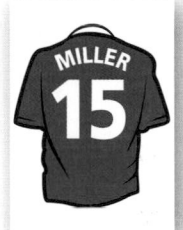  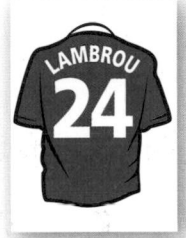

- Find the mean average of your cards, by adding the numbers together and dividing by 4.

  7 + 15 + 9 + 24 = 55   55 ÷ 4 = 13.75

- The player with the higher mean average scores a goal.
- Round 2: both players should pick 5 cards.

   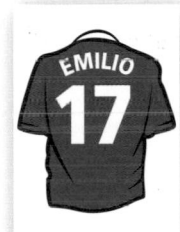 

- Find the mean average of your cards, by adding the numbers together and dividing by 5.

  5 + 22 + 11 + 17 + 3 = 58   58 ÷ 5 = 11.6

- You may use a calculator if you need to for the dividing but not for the adding!
- Continue in this way, picking 6, then 7 and finally 8 cards for the next three rounds.
- The winner is the player with the most goals at the end.

Manager's Message
Remember that you should always divide by the number of cards you have.

Pick two

Resources: pack of Shelby Town cards

- Play this game in two teams.
- Player 1 from each team chooses two cards, e.g. 2 and 18, 5 and 17.

- The teams must divide the larger card by the smaller card to see if the answer is a whole number, e.g. Does 2 divide into 18? 2, 4, 6, 8, 12, 14, 16, 18 – yes! So 18 is a multiple of 2.
- The team scores a goal if one number is a multiple of the other, e.g. 2 and 18. If not, e.g. 5 and 17, the team does not score.
- Replace any card under 7 back into the pack after each turn.
- Players take it in turns to pick two cards.
- The winning team is the one that scores the most goals.

Sum match

Resources: pack of Shelby Town cards

- Play this game in two teams.
- Each team picks two cards without looking at them and finds the total of their two numbers.
- The team with the larger total scores a goal. If the totals are equal, no one scores.
- Next, pick three cards and find the total. Again, the team with the larger total sores a goal.
- Keep on playing in this way until you pick up 12 cards or are no longer able to work out the totals.
- The winning team is the one that scores the most goals.

Manager's Message
Think of strategies to help
you find the total as you play.